Eyewitness
MYTHOLOGY

The Wealthy One (1988), a contemporary Native American mask

Monstrous Chimera

Maori ceremonial adze (ax)

Hideous gorgon Medusa

Ritual sword used in Ogun worship

Hindu animal god Garuda

Mold and casting of Venus, Roman goddess of love

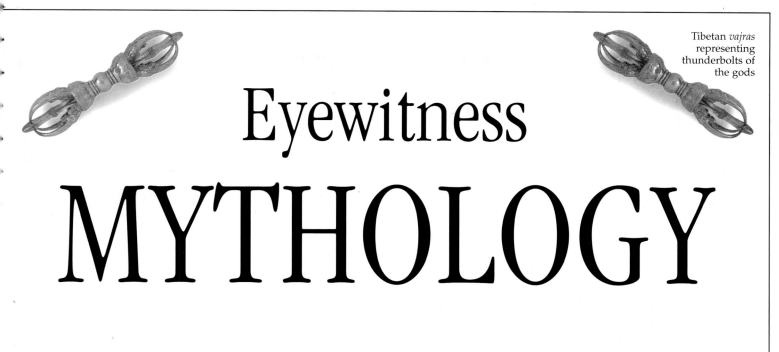

Tibetan *vajras* representing thunderbolts of the gods

Eyewitness
MYTHOLOGY

Written by
NEIL PHILIP

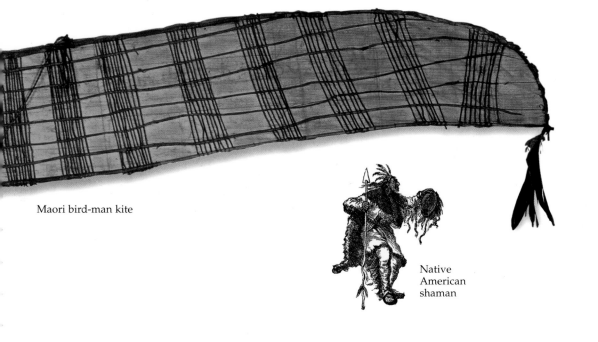

Maori bird-man kite

Native American shaman

DK

DK Publishing, Inc.

Japanese
prayer
offerings

African fortune-telling
cowrie shells

Tangaroa, supreme god of Polynesia

Oceanic
ceremonial
ax

Staff representing
African thunder
god Shango's ax

Back of Tangaroa

DK

LONDON, NEW YORK, MUNICH,
MELBOURNE, and DELHI

Project editor Melanie Halton
Art editor Joanne Connor
Senior managing editor Linda Martin
Senior managing art editor Julia Harris
Production Kate Oliver
Picture research Andy Sansom
DTP designer Andrew O'Brien

REVISED EDITION
Managing editor Linda Esposito
Senior editor Shaila Awan
Managing art editor Jane Thomas
Category publisher Linda Martin
Art director Simon Webb
Editor and reference compiler Clare Hibbert
Art editor Rebecca Johns
Consultant Neil Philip
Production Jenny Jacoby
Picture research Carolyn Clerkin, Harriet Mills
DTP designer Siu Yin Ho

U.S. editors Elizabeth Hester, John Searcy
Publishing director Beth Sutinis
Art director Dirk Kaufman
U.S. DTP designer Milos Orlovic
U.S. production Chris Avgherinos, Ivor Parker

This Eyewitness ® Guide has been conceived by
Dorling Kindersley Limited and Editions Gallimard

This edition published in the United States in 2005
by DK Publishing, Inc.
375 Hudson Street, New York, NY 10014

07 08 09 10 9 8 7 6 5

A catalog record for this book is
available from the Library of Congress.
ISBN-13: 978-0-7566-1079-1 (PLC)
ISBN-13: 978-0-7566-1080-7 (ALB)
Color reproduction by
Colourscan, Singapore
Printed in China by Toppan Co.,
(Shenzhen) Ltd.

Discover more at
www.dk.com

Contents

Navajo
sandpainting

Sandpainting
pigments

What is mythology?

THE WORD "MYTH" comes from the Greek *mythos*, meaning a word or a story. Sometimes it is used to mean something that people believe that is not true: "It's a myth that carrots help you see in the dark." But mythology is not a collection of lies; it is a collection of truths. Each human culture makes stories about the creation of the world, the origins of humankind, and the meaning of life. These stories are myths. Mythology puts across religious ideas in the form of stories. But while the essence of religious belief is usually very simple, mythology can be highly complex. This is because myths are stories that explore rather than explain. They show the human mind searching to balance the forces of creation and destruction, of life and death.

Long-haired figures represent the shaman wrestling with the beaver

CREATION OF THE WORLD
Numerous mythologies tell how the creator emerged from a cosmic egg or a primordial (existing from the beginning) ocean. The world was then brought into being, perhaps from the creator's own body, perhaps from mud, or even by the power of words or thought. The first Hindu god, Brahma, is sometimes said to have been born from a golden egg that floated on the first waters.

Hindu creation symbol

Myth beginnings

Humankind has made myths from the dawn of history. The oldest living mythology is that of the Australian Aborigines, whose stories of the sacred eternal Dreamtime, or Dreaming, stretch back 40,000 years. The myths of diverse cultures are often linked by similar themes. This timeline shows the approximate dates that individual societies began recording or shaping their myths.

Burning stick symbolizes the beaver's magic powers

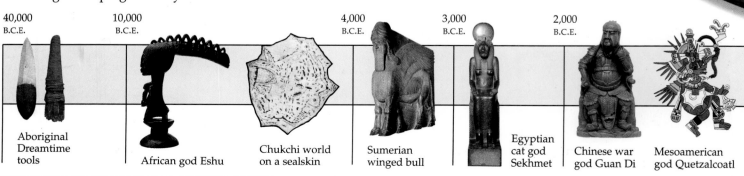

40,000 B.C.E.	10,000 B.C.E.		4,000 B.C.E.	3,000 B.C.E.	2,000 B.C.E.	
Aboriginal Dreamtime tools	African god Eshu	Chukchi world on a sealskin	Sumerian winged bull	Egyptian cat god Sekhmet	Chinese war god Guan Di	Mesoamerican god Quetzalcoatl

GUIDING ANCESTORS

Ancestors play an important role in world mythology. For the Australian Aborigines, the laws and customs established by ancestor spirits (left) act as guidelines for life today. These ancestors exist outside time, in the eternal present of the Dreamtime. Aboriginal myths are stories of the Dreamtime, and Aboriginal art and ceremonies are ways of connecting with the ancestors.

CHALLENGING THE GODS

Not all are content to worship the gods; some even challenge them. When Nimrod, King of Babylon, built a tower to reach heaven and make war on God, God sent 70 angels to confuse the builders' tongues. Some say that this is why people now speak different languages.

The Tower of Babel fell when the workmen could no longer understand each other

STORYTELLING

Myths are passed on by storytelling, not only by word of mouth and in writing, but also in rituals, dances, dramas, and artworks. This *Medicine Beaver* mask tells the story of the life-or-death struggle between a North American Nisga-a shaman, or medicine man, and a giant beaver, in which the shaman made the beaver into his spirit helper.

PERSEPHONE AND HADES

Many mythologies hope for a new life after death. The Egyptians and the Greeks both linked the idea of an afterlife with the annual death and resurrection of wheat. The Greeks worshiped Persephone, daughter of the wheat goddess Demeter, as queen of the dead, in rites that they believed held the entire human race together.

	1,000 B.C.E.					1 C.E.		1,000 C.E.
Hindu figure of Garuda		Bible story of Adam and Eve	Polynesian god Tangaroa	Greek supreme god Zeus	Celtic horned god Cernunnos	Roman war god Mars		Norse god Thor's hammer	Japanese prayer offerings

Creation of the world

COSMIC EGG
A bird-man from Rapa Nui (Easter Island) is shown holding the cosmic egg that contains the world. Each year in the nesting season, the man whose servant was the first to gather an egg became Rapa Nui's Bird Man, the living representative for that year of the creator god Makemake.

MANY PEOPLES seem to agree that this world was made as a deliberate act of creation by a divine being. Often the world is described as having originally been all ocean, and it is from the sea that the world emerges in the earliest mythologies. Nun was the god of the Egyptian primal ocean. The Arctic Tikigak people say that Raven made the land by harpooning a great whale, which then floated and became dry land. Sometimes there are two creators, who together shape the world, such as First Creator and Lone Man of the Native American Mandan tribe. They sent a mud hen down to fetch mud from the bottom of the flood to make the first land.

FIRE AND ICE
The Vikings believed that the world began when fire from the south met ice from the north. At the center, the ice began to thaw and, as it dripped, it shaped itself into the first being, Ymir, whose sweat formed the first frost giants. Then the ice-melt shaped a cow, whose milk fed Ymir. As the cow licked the ice, she shaped the first man, Buri.

Pottery figurine of Gaea from Thebes, 450 B.C.

FLOATING DISK
According to the ancient Greeks, the first to be born from the primeval chaos was Gaea, the Earth. The Earth was conceived as a disk floating on a waste of waters, and encircled by the river Oceanus. Gaea gave birth to Uranus, the sky, and Cronus (time).

Ahura Mazda, from the tree of life relief, 9th century B.C.

THE BIG BANG
Scientists now say that the world began with the Big Bang, a huge explosion 13 billion years ago that sent matter in all directions to create the ever-expanding Universe. This is a new vision of beginning; a new "myth" for a scientific age.

CREATED FROM GOODNESS
The ancient Persians believed in twin spirits who had existed since the beginning of time: Ahura Mazda, who was good; and Ahriman, who was evil. It was Ahura Mazda who created the physical world, set time in motion, and created humankind.

TURTLE ISLAND
Many Native Americans believe that this world is supported on a turtle's back. According to the Seneca tribe, when the first woman fell down from another world in the sky, the toad that lived on the primal waters dived down to fetch mud to place on the turtle's back. The mud, which became Earth, provided support for the first woman.

The first land was said to have been created on a turtle's back

19th-century Native American Cheyenne shield

CURDLING OCEAN
The Japanese god Izanagi and his wife Izanami stood on the floating bridge of heaven and stirred the ocean with a jeweled spear until it curdled and formed the first island, Onokoro. They built a house there, with a central stone pillar that is the backbone of the world.

Vishnu sits on top of Mount Mandara

OCEAN CHURNING
At the beginning of this cycle of creation, a number of vital treasures, including the elixir of immortality, were not to be found, so the Hindu gods decided to churn the ocean, using Mount Mandara as the paddle. As they churned, the ocean turned to milk, then to butter, and the Sun and Moon arose. As they churned some more, the elixir was finally created.

Vasuki, the cosmic serpent, was used as a rope to twist the mountain

The mountain is supported by a giant turtle

The Milky Way and the planets of the Solar System. Clockwise from the bottom are the Earth, Mars, Jupiter, Saturn, Uranus, and Neptune.

The cosmos

PEOPLE HAVE ALWAYS WONDERED about the mysteries of the world, from its origin and shape to its cosmos, or order. The world is often thought to have emerged from a cosmic egg. In China, the warring forces of yin and yang in the egg created the first being, Pan Gu. The Dogon of West Africa believe the world was formed from a vibrating egg that burst open to reveal a creator spirit. The Ainu of Japan believed there were six skies above this Earth and six worlds below it, the abodes of gods, demons, and animals. The world has long been thought of as round. A myth told by the Inuit people of the Arctic tundra tells how two families set out in opposite directions to discover how big the world is. When they met up again, they were very old, but the fact that they came back to where they started proved that the world is round. The Mangaian people of Polynesia say that the universe is held in the shell of a huge coconut.

Inuit people of the Arctic tundra build an igloo, which is round like the world

WORLD IN A SEALSKIN
On this sealskin painted by the Chukchi people of Siberia, the whole Arctic world – Sun, Moon, land, sea, and sky – is captured in a small space. Human beings share creation with spirits, animals, and gods such as the creator Raven and his wife, Miti, and Sedna, the mother of the sea beasts.

YIN AND YANG
The Chinese believed that the first being, Pan Gu, was created inside a cosmic egg by the opposing forces of yin and yang. When at last the conflict between yin and yang broke the egg open, Pan Gu was born and pushed the sky away from the Earth.
After he died, exhausted by this labor, his body formed the mountains and the land — and his fleas became humankind.

Yin and yang symbolize universal opposites, such as good and evil, that must be equally balanced for a harmonious world

Brahma, the creator of the Universe, is shown on Vishnu's forehead

Vishnu's conch shell symbolizes the very first vibration of the Universe — the sound "om"

The discus symbolizes the mind and the sun

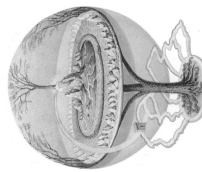

WORLD TREE
For the Vikings the nine worlds, including humankind's "middle Earth," were arranged in three layers around the huge ash tree Yggdrasil, which stands at the center of the cosmos. The Vikings believed that the worlds of gods, giants, elves, dwarfs, humans, and the dead were all sustained by the world tree.

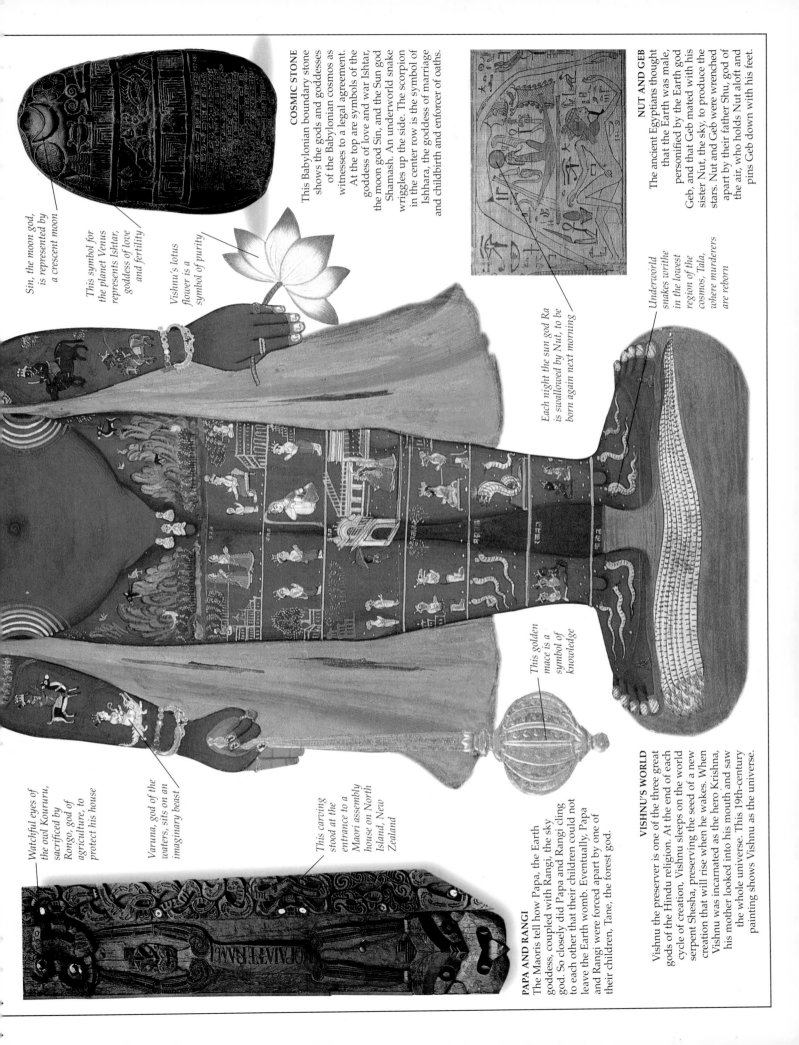

COSMIC STONE

This Babylonian boundary stone shows the gods and goddesses of the Babylonian cosmos as witnesses to a legal agreement. At the top are symbols of the goddess of love and war Ishtar, the moon god Sin, and the Sun god Shamash. An underworld snake wriggles up the side. The scorpion in the center row is the symbol of Ishhara, the goddess of marriage and childbirth and enforcer of oaths.

Sin, the moon god, is represented by a crescent moon

This symbol for the planet Venus represents Ishtar, goddess of love and fertility

Vishnu's lotus flower is a symbol of purity

NUT AND GEB

The ancient Egyptians thought that the Earth was male, personified by the Earth god Geb, and that Geb mated with his sister Nut, the sky, to produce the stars. Nut and Geb were wrenched apart by their father Shu, god of the air, who holds Nut aloft and pins Geb down with his feet.

Underworld snakes writhe in the lowest region of the cosmos, Tala, where murderers are reborn

Each night the sun god Ra is swallowed by Nut, to be born again next morning

This golden mace is a symbol of knowledge

Watchful eyes of the owl Koururu, sacrificed by Rongo, god of agriculture, to protect his house

Varuna, god of the waters, sits on an imaginary beast

This carving stood at the entrance to a Maori assembly house on North Island, New Zealand

PAPA AND RANGI

The Maoris tell how Papa, the Earth goddess, coupled with Rangi, the sky god. So closely did Papa and Rangi cling to each other that their children could not leave the Earth womb. Eventually, Papa and Rangi were forced apart by one of their children, Tane, the forest god.

VISHNU'S WORLD

Vishnu the preserver is one of the three great gods of the Hindu religion. At the end of each cycle of creation, Vishnu sleeps on the world serpent Shesha, preserving the seed of a new creation that will rise when he wakes. When Vishnu was incarnated as the hero Krishna, his mother looked into his mouth and saw the whole universe. This 19th-century painting shows Vishnu as the universe.

Sun and Moon

THE SUN AND THE MOON, which light up the sky by day and night and enable us to tell the time, have been the subject of many myths. For the Native American Zuni people, Moonlight-Giving Mother and Sun Father are the givers of light and life. The Native American Cherokees say the sun is female and tell of her grief when her daughter died from a rattlesnake bite. Sun hid herself away, the world grew dark, and her tears caused a flood. Only the dancing and singing of young men and women could cheer her up. The Arctic Chukchi tell how a woman married the sun, but a black beetle took her place; it was only when her son sought out his father that the imposter was discovered. Another Chukchi woman married the moon; she had been deserted by her husband and left to starve, but she crawled to moon's house and became his wife.

DEALER OF DAYS
The moon god Thoth was in charge of the Egyptian calendar, which had 12 months with 30 days each. The sky goddess Nut, who had been cursed so that she could never give birth, won five extra days from Thoth in which she had her children.

THE ROMAN GODDESS DIANA
Diana (Artemis in Greek) is shown here with her foot resting on the Moon, with which she was closely associated. More often, however, she is depicted with a crescent Moon in her hair.

Diana as a crowned moon goddess

The face on this Inuit mask represents the spirit of the moon

Decorative feathers represent the stars

White border around the face symbolizes air

FEEDING HUMANKIND
The Inuit moon man is called Igaluk or Tarqeq. Shamans make spirit journeys to ask him to promise that he will send animals for men to hunt. The moon man also helps the souls of the dead to be reborn as humans, animals, or fish.

Painted moon face sculpted in wood

Native American Haida mask

POLLUTING THE WORLD
A Native American Haida myth tells how Wultcixaiya, the son of the moon, rescued his sister from her unhappy marriage to Pestilence. Wearing a steel coat, he broke into Pestilence's house of rock, freeing her, but also polluting the world with sickness and disease.

SUN GOD RA
The falcon-headed god Horus joined forces with the Egyptian Sun god Ra and became Ra-Horakhty. He sailed a special boat, the *Solar Barque*, across the sky by day and through the underworld by night.

The Sun's rays beam down on a worshiper

Projections symbolize the Sun's rays

INCA INTI
Viracocha, the Inca creator god, ordered the Sun, Moon, and stars to emerge from the Island of the Sun, in Lake Titicaca, to bring light to the world. Inti, the Sun god, was regarded as the father of the Inca emperors, and his wife, Mama Kilya, the moon goddess, as the mother of the Inca race.

Pre-Columbian gold sun mask, 300 B.C.E

CHILDREN OF THE SUN
The Native American Tsimshian hero Asdiwal was a great hunter, who pursued a bear right up to the sky. The bear turned out to be the Sun's beautiful daughter, whom Asdiwal married. The Sun also has a son, a shining prince of the sky, who had a constant battle of wits with his cheeky servant.

Tsimshian chief's ceremonial headdress representing the Sun

The fertility goddess Ishtar

Ea, the water god

Shamash rising between two mountains

ENEMY OF DARKNESS
The Babylonian Sun god Shamash was the only being able to cross the ocean of death, until the hero Gilgamesh. Shamash was a lawgiver and healer, the enemy of darkness, wrongdoing, and disease.

Amaterasu holds the imperial sword and necklace

SUN GODDESS AMATERASU
The Japanese Sun goddess Amaterasu was so offended by her brother Susano's practical jokes that she hid in a cave and deprived the world of the Sun. Uzume, the goddess of mirth, did a striptease and made the other gods laugh. Intrigued, Amaterasu emerged from the cave, returning sunlight to the world.

Making humankind

ALL MYTHOLOGIES TELL how the first human beings were made. Often the creator shaped them from clay or mud. The Unalit (North Alaskan Inuit) say that the first man was born from the pod of a beach pea. When he burst out of the pod, he was met by Raven, who taught him how to live and made him a wife out of clay. The Egyptians believed that the first human beings were made from the tears of Ra, the sun god. For the Serbians, people were made from the creator's sweat, which is why they say we are doomed to a life of toil. The Norse god Odin made the first man and woman from driftwood, but there is also a myth telling how the Norse god Heimdall fathered the various kinds of men: serfs, warriors, and kings.

Brahma has four heads so that he can see in all directions

BRAHMA THE CREATOR
The Hindu creator Brahma is the universal soul, the "self-existent great-grandfather." He made the world and everything in it. He is sometimes called Purusha, the first being. As Purusha he divided himself into two, male and female, and coupled in the form of every creature, from humans to ants.

Tangaroa brings forth other beings

Carved wooden bowl from the Yoruba in West Africa

The cosmic serpent Aido-Hwedo coiled itself around the Earth

BODIES OF CLAY
The West African creator Mawu made the first people from clay and water. The first man and woman, sometimes called Adanhu and Yewa, were sent down from the sky with the rainbow serpent Aido-Hwedo. For the first 17 days it did nothing but rain; the man and woman did not speak but only called out the name of the god who had sent them to Earth.

Adanhu

Yewa

Wooden statue from the Tubuaï Islands in Polynesia, where the supreme god Tangaroa is called A'a

Wooden idols

FIRST HUMANS
When the statue of Tangaroa (left) was first discovered, it contained wooden idols like these, which represented the first men and women.

New beings crawl on Tangaroa's back

POTTER'S PEOPLE
The Egyptian ram-god Khnum was the potter who shaped each human being and their ka, or life force, on his potter's wheel. He was worshiped at the island of Elephantine, with his wife, Satet, and their daughter Anuket, the huntress. An inscription on a block of granite found at Elephantine records how prayers to Khnum brought to an end a seven-year famine.

Tangaroa's body cavity contained wooden idols

The tree of the knowledge of good and evil

WOODEN STATUES
Tangaroa (Ta'aroa) is the Polynesian god of the ocean. In some places he is considered the maker of all things. In Tahiti it is said that Tangaroa lived inside the cosmic egg at the beginning of time. When he broke out, he called, "Who's there?" but there was no reply. So Tangaroa created the world and called forth gods and humans from his body.

Tangaroa creates other gods and humankind

ADAM AND EVE
According to the Bible, God created Adam, the first man, in his own image. He shaped him out of clay and made Eve, the first woman, from one of Adam's ribs to be his companion. Islamic tradition says that when God breathed life into Adam's nostrils, he sneezed and said, "Praise be to Allah."

Supreme beings

M OST MYTHOLOGIES tell of one god who reigns supreme over all others. These supreme gods may be associated with the creation of the world and humankind. Many supreme deities, such as the Greek god Zeus, are essentially sky gods; others may be Sun, battle, city, or tribal gods. In some cultures, especially in Africa, the supreme god is thought to have retired from the world after the initial creation. This is the case with Nana-Buluku, the creator deity of the Fon of West Africa; and with Nyame of the West African Ashanti people. Over time such gods may be almost forgotten. For instance, Nana-Buluku's daughter Mawu is now routinely described as the creator, and the word "mawu" has come to mean "god" in Fon.

Thunderbolts were made for Zeus by the Cyclopes, giants who helped in the war against Zeus's father

RULER OF THE GREEKS
Zeus (known as Jupiter to the Romans) was ruler of the Greek gods. Zeus overthrew his father, Cronos, before establishing his rule on Mount Olympus. His wife, Hera, goddess of marriage, was jealous because of his many love affairs, during which he fathered the gods Apollo and Artemis, and the heroes Perseus and Heracles (or Hercules).

Made of bronze and decorated with silver, this late Bronze Age figure represents the storm god Baal

THE RAINMAKER
The Canaanite storm god Baal made thunder with his mace and produced lightning from his lance. Baal revolted against El, his father, by defeating El's favorite, Yam, the god of the sea. Another myth tells of his long battle against Mot, god of death.

BABYLONIAN KING OF THE GODS
This doglike dragon is the symbol of Marduk, the Babylonian king of the gods. Strong and heroic, he was given authority over the other gods, including his father, Ea, the god of wisdom, when he agreed to slay the dragon Tiamat (one of two primal beings). Marduk created humankind from the blood of Tiamat's son Kingu.

FEATHERED SERPENT
Half-snake, half-bird, Quetzalcoatl was the Aztec lord of life and god of the winds. He descended to the underworld to retrieve the bones of early humans in order to create new beings. The underworld was ruled by his father, the death god Mictlantecuhtli.

The feathers of more than 250 quetzal birds make up this headdress

Aztec serpent god Quetzalcoatl

Headdress of Montezuma II, the last Aztec ruler

Wooden kantele from Karelia in Finland, 1893

Stoneware Taoist shrine of the Ming dynasty, 1406 A.D.

Lao-tzu, the founder of Taoism, is shown riding a buffalo

SINGING SHAMAN
Vainamoinen, the eternal singer, was the son of the Finnish air-goddess Ilmatar. He was born old, so no one wanted to marry him — one girl, Aino, even became a mermaid rather than be his bride. Vainamoinen was a shaman, whose songs to the sound of his harplike kantele were acts of creative magic.

The Jade Emperor

LORD OF THE HEAVENS
The Chinese gods formed a huge bureaucracy, at the head of which was the Jade Emperor. He was assisted by the God of the Eastern Peak, who had no fewer than 75 departments under his control, each supervised by lesser gods. The Jade Emperor's wife was Xi Wang Mu, the Queen Mother of the West, guardian of the peaches of immortality, which she served at a great feast once every 1,000 years.

Ebony mortar and pestle from Tanzania, East Africa

Mortar

Pestle

The God of the Eastern Peak

STAIRWAY TO HEAVEN
Nyame is the sky god of the Ashanti of Africa. He used to live close to humans, but when an old woman annoyed him by knocking him with her pestle as she pounded yams, he moved away toward the heavens. The old woman and her sons tried to reach him by piling mortars on top of each other, but they were one short. They took the mortar from the bottom to place it on the top, and the pile collapsed, killing them all.

Floods and storms

THE STORY OF A GREAT FLOOD that once overwhelmed the Earth – a flood that only a lucky few survived – is one of the most widespread of all myths. The earliest flood story is found in the Mesopotamian epic of Gilgamesh, in which Utnapishtim frees birds to see if the waters are subsiding. The Native American Mandan tribe spoke of Lone Man, who survived a great flood in his big canoe. The Greek god Zeus, tired of the wickedness of humans, sent a flood to drown them all. But the giant Prometheus warned his son Deucalion, who built an ark in time to save himself and his wife.

SAVED BY A FISH
One day the Hindu sage Manu found a fish in his washing water. The fish told Manu that he should build a ship because a great flood was coming. When the flood arrived, the fish, which was an incarnation of the Hindu god Vishnu, towed Manu to safety. Manu then became the father of all humankind.

Giant Wave, a print of a tsunami (huge, violent wave) by Katsushika Hokusai (1760–1849)

A tsunami is usually caused by an earthquake or a volcano; here, a tsunami batters a Japanese plank boat

KINGDOM OF ATLANTIS
Poseidon, the Greek god of the sea, fell in love with a woman called Clito and built her a paradise island. Clito bore Poseidon sons, who founded the kingdom of Atlantis on the island. The brothers ruled the island in wisdom. But later rulers became greedy and corrupt, so Poseidon sent a tidal wave to swallow up Atlantis and all its people.

Headdress of tropical bird feathers

Type of poncho worn by Sapa Incas, the first of whom named himself after the supreme god Viracocha

In his left hand, Chac carries a bowl; in his right, a ball of smoking incense

MAYAN RAINMAKER
Chac, the rain god, broke open a great rock to uncover the first corn plant. And it was Chac who sent the rain each year to enable the corn to grow. But sometimes, instead of gentle rain, Chac sent violent storms, in which he wielded his weapon, lightning.

GIANT WAVES
The great flood is caused either by a deluge of rain, as in the Noah story (below), or by a gigantic tidal wave that sweeps over the land, as in the story of Atlantis (above). Both are terrifying images of unstoppable destruction.

CREATOR OF HUMANS
Viracocha, the Inca creator god, was displeased with his first attempt at creating humans from stone, so he drowned them all in a flood. He then tried again, this time making the people from clay. He wandered among these new people as a beggar, teaching them how to live.

NOAH AND THE ARK
When God saw how wicked humans had become, he decided to drown them all, for he was sorry he had ever created them. But he decided to save one good man, Noah. He warned Noah to build an ark in which to save his family and two of every living creature to people the Earth after the great flood. When the flooding subsided, God set the rainbow in the sky as a promise that he would never again destroy humanity by a flood.

Some believe that gods live at the peak of Mount Fuji in Japan, which is always capped with snow

The elements

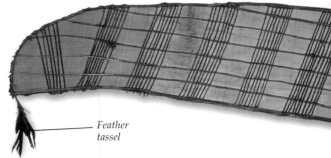

Feather tassel

ALL OVER the world, the elemental forces that form it have been the focus of myth-making. Fire, air, earth, and water are the "four elements" in Western tradition. The Chinese have five elements: wood, fire, earth, metal, and water. Almost all mythologies tell how humans acquired the gift of fire, often stolen from the sun. Gods of the air and the sky have been so important that the names of many supreme gods, such as the Greek Zeus, simply mean "sky." The Earth, though sometimes regarded as male, is more often thought of as our mother. According to the mythology of ancient Babylon, in the beginning nothing existed but Apsu, the freshwater ocean; and Tiamat, the saltwater ocean. These two waters have given and taken life since the dawn of time.

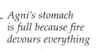

Agni's stomach is full because fire devours everything

FIRE-EATER
Wherever a fire is lit, the Hindu fire god Agni is born. Because he is present in all homes, he knows all secrets. He once helped a man find his wife, who had been carried away by the sage Bhrigu. Bhrigu then cursed Agni, making him consume all the dirt of the Earth. But as Agni devours the dirt, he also purifies it with his flames.

VOLCANIC PELE
In Hawaii, which is dominated by the Kilauea volcano, Pele is worshiped as the goddess of fire. She is as passionate and dangerous as a volcano. She fell in love with the prince of Kauai, but when he preferred her sister, she encased him in molten lava and turned him to stone.

OCEANS OF OLOKUN
Olokun, the sea king of the Edo people of Benin, Nigeria, is a powerful god. He is the source of all wealth and the bringer of children, whose souls must cross the ocean to be born. His palace is a paradise, full of the noise of children, and his wives, who are the rivers. The Olokun river is the source of all the waters of the Earth, including the ocean.

Mother-of-pearl eyes embedded in a painted face

Kite is made of canvas and twigs

SKY MAN

Tawhaki, the great Polynesian hero whom the Maori call the god of thunder and lightning, ascended to the sky world as a kite, seeking to avenge his father, Hema, whose eyes had been gouged out by goblins to use as lights. Maori priests foretold the future by watching the dance of kites in the air.

Balls of rolling thunder

The thunder god is depicted as a demon in the air

Maori kite in the form of a bird with a human head

Drumstick makes the thunder

EARTH MOTHER

Toci, mother of the gods, was an important Aztec earth goddess. She was a goddess of the harvest, of childbirth, and of curing, but also of war and discord. The Earth itself was said to have been made by the gods from the body of the fearsome goddess Tlaltecuhtli, who could be appeased only by being given human hearts to eat.

Aztec earth goddess (A.D. 1300–1521)

Poseidon's trident, a three-pronged fisherman's spear

THUNDER ROLLS

This burly Japanese god (possibly Kami-Nari, the god of rolling thunder) beats out thunder on his drum. Japanese thunder deities are threatening forces. When Izanagi, the primal male, descended to hell in search of his wife, the decomposing goddess sent eight thunder gods to chase him from the underworld.

STORMY SEAS

Poseidon, the Greek god of the sea, had a violent and vengeful nature. This showed in his persecution of the hero Odysseus, who had blinded the god's son. As well as causing storms at sea, Poseidon was also believed to cause earthquakes.

Japanese thunder god

Aboriginal stone ax from Northern Territory, Australia

LIGHTNING MAN

The Lightning Brothers are important ancestor figures in the Dreamtime of the Aborigines of Australia's Northern Territory. Tcabuinji killed his younger brother, Wagtjadbulla, with a stone ax in an argument about Tcabuinji's wife. It is this ax that Tcabuinji uses to split trees when lightning strikes.

The natural world

ALL THE ELEMENTS OF THE NATURAL WORLD — animals, flowers, plants, and trees — are the gifts of the gods and remain in their care. Many cultures worshiped the Earth as a mother goddess, provider of food and fertility. But they also gave responsibility for important crops — such as maize for Native Americans, or rice for the Japanese — to specific gods or goddesses. Hunting societies believe that game is withheld or released by divinities such as Sedna, the North American Inuit mistress of the sea beasts. In the forests of northern Cameroon, hunters pray to the Bedimo, ancestral spirits, to release game from their divine stables.

Spanish reed

This type of reed has been used to make pipes for 5,000 years

PAN'S PIPES
With his goatlike horns and legs, Pan was the Greek god of the pastures, especially of sheep and goats. He could inspire fear in his enemies, who would flee in what we now call a "panic." Pan was also very amorous. One nymph, Syrinx, turned into reeds to escape him. But Pan made himself a set of musical pipes from the reeds so that she would always be close to him.

Cobs of corn

SPRINGTIME GOD
The Aztec god of spring, Xipec Totec, allowed his skin to be flayed (peeled off) in order to promote new growth from within — like a corn seed breaking through its husk to become a new plant. At festivals in his honor, young men wore the skins of human sacrificial offerings.

Farmers harvesting rice

RICE SUPPLIES
Every village in Japan has a shrine dedicated to the rice god Inari, who comes down from his mountain home in the spring and returns in the autumn, after the rice harvest.

Rice grains

Wooden mask representing
the nature spirits of the
North American Inuits

Kelp
seaweed

MOTHER OF SEA BEASTS

Sedna, the Inuit sea woman,
was thrown into the sea by
her father because she married
a dog. When she tried to cling
to the kayak (boat), he chopped
off her fingers, which turned
into the first sea mammals. To
show her appreciation for the
help given her by humans,
who comb her hair, Sedna
releases the sea beasts so
that humankind can feed.

*Mask represents the various sea
beasts, such as seals and fish,
that Sedna watches over*

*This Maori ceremonial
adze (axlike tool)
symbolizes Tane, who
was himself shaped by
craftsmen with adzes*

TANE OF THE TREES

The Oceanic forest god Tane
lived in the highest heaven,
from which he brought down
three baskets of knowledge for
humankind. He made himself a
wife, Hine-hau-one (the Earth-
formed maiden), from red
sand. Their daughter, the
dawn maiden, ran away to
become Hine-nui-te-Po,
the goddess of death.

*Flora awakens
the flowers
with her
sweet music*

FLOWERING FLORA

Flora was the Roman goddess of the
flowers, who made plants and trees
bloom. Flora also had a flower which
made women pregnant when they
touched it. She lent the flower to the
goddess Juno, who soon became
pregnant with Mars, the god of war.

Celtic bronze horse found in the tomb of a prince (c. 5th century B.C.)

EQUESTRIAN EPONA
Epona, the Celtic horse goddess, is closely linked to the triple mother goddesses, who are often shown nursing babies. Like them, Epona is often shown with wheat and other fertility symbols, but she was especially associated with horse breeding. Horse breeding was crucial because the Celts farmed with horses, and without them could not have grown enough food.

Fertility and birth

WORSHIP OF THE GREAT MOTHER goddess, often identified as the Earth, has been part of many religions since the dawn of humanity. For instance, Pacha Mama, the name of the Inca fertility goddess, means "earth mother." When the Hittite god of farming, Telepinu, withdrew from the world in a rage, and humans began to starve, it was the mother goddess Hannahanna who found him. The myth of the Greek corn goddess Demeter and her despairing search for her lost daughter Persephone, during which the Earth became a wasteland, was at the heart of Greek religion. Birth and fertility were not exclusively the reserve of goddesses. Frey was the Norse god of fertility, a role given in Egypt to the gods Min and Osiris; Egyptian mothers wanted the aid of the impish god Bes at childbirth.

FREY AND FREYA
Twin brother and sister Frey and Freya were Norse fertility gods. Frey's cult involved his image being carried from place to place in a wagon during the winter months to ensure fertility. Freya, who was considered to be the most beautiful of all goddesses, was primarily the goddess of love and of soothsaying (predicting the future).

Goddess Freya in her chariot

Frey holds his beard, a symbol of growth, in one hand

JADE SKIRT
Chalchiuhtlicue, "she of the jade skirt," was the central Mexican goddess of lakes and streams and, by association, the goddess of birth. She is sometimes depicted with a pair of babies, one male and one female. Chalchiuhtlicue once flooded the Earth but turned humankind into fish so that they were saved.

The water goddess Chalchiutlicue stands in water near a giant centipede

Native American Iroquois corn husk mask, worn in midwinter ceremonies to ensure a good harvest

Alabaster figurine of Ishtar c. 300–200 B.C.

Baby Horus

LOVE GODDESS
Ishtar, the Babylonian goddess of love, descended to the underworld to rescue her dead husband Tammuz, god of plants. But she was killed and, without Tammuz, the whole world withered. Ishtar was brought back to life, but for six months of each year Tammuz must live in the underworld, while Ishtar laments; when he rises in the spring, all rejoice.

ISIS AND HORUS
The Egyptian goddess Isis is often shown as the perfect mother, nursing the infant Horus. When he was only a baby, Horus was bitten by scorpions and would have died, but Isis's cries of anguish halted the sun god Ra in his journey across the sky. Ra then sent the god Thoth to cure the child.

FIRST MOTHER
Native Americans of the Northeast tell how First Father was born from the foam on the sea, and First Mother from the dew on the leaf. The human race increased, but eventually came a time of famine. Then First Mother, who had said, "My strength shall be felt all over the Earth," asked to be killed and buried. From her flesh grew the first wheat.

Mold for making the casting of Venus (right)

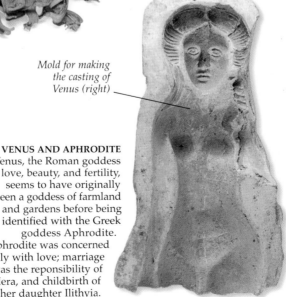

WILLENDORF VENUS
This stone Venus figurine from Willendorf, in Austria, represents a goddess and dates from the neolithic period (c. 5,000 B.C.). The exaggerated curves in this statue of the great mother goddess stress women's role in human fertility.

VENUS AND APHRODITE
Venus, the Roman goddess of love, beauty, and fertility, seems to have originally been a goddess of farmland and gardens before being identified with the Greek goddess Aphrodite. Aphrodite was concerned only with love; marriage was the reponsibility of Hera, and childbirth of her daughter Ilithyia.

Children of the gods

IN MANY MYTHOLOGIES, THE GODS reproduce just as human beings do. Their children may be other gods (who may even take over from them), or semidivine heroes, such as Cuchulain and Hercules. Some supreme deities, such as the Norse god Odin and the Greek god Zeus, are called "all-father" in recognition of the role they play for other beings. However, not all children of the gods are beneficial to the world. For instance, the Norse god Loki gave birth to the fierce wolf Fenrir and Hel, the mistress of the underworld; the Greek god of the sea, Poseidon, fathered the brutal Cyclops Polyphemus. Gods can also incarnate themselves in human or animal form, as the Hindu god Vishnu does in his various guises, such as Narasimba, the half-man, half-lion; and Vamana, the dwarf.

Matsya, the fish

Kurma, the turtle

INCARNATIONS OF VISHNU
The Hindu god Vishnu, the preserver, has been incarnated nine times in different forms. As the fish, Vishnu saved Manu, the first man, from the great flood. As the turtle, he helped the gods churn the ocean and win the elixir of immortality. Vishnu raised the Earth out of the sea as Varaha the boar. And as the hero Rama, he rescued his wife from a demon. Vishnu's tenth avatar, Kalki, the horse, will come to destroy and re-create the world at the end of this cycle of time.

Varaha, the boar

FATHER OF THE PHARAOHS
Falcon-headed Horus, whose eyes were the sun and the moon, was the child of the Egyptian gods Isis and Osiris. He was conceived when Isis breathed life into the mummified Osiris, who had been murdered by his brother Seth. The long battle between Horus and Seth was vicious, but eventually Horus prevailed. The Egyptian pharaohs traced their descent from him and were called the "living Horus."

Cuchulain rides his chariot into battle

UGLY WARRIOR
Cuchulain, a hero of Irish mythology, was a fierce warrior. His father was the sun god Lugh. Although normally very handsome, on the battlefield Cuchulain became a monster. One eye disappeared into his head, the other bulged; his heels turned to the front; and his jaws opened wide enough to swallow an enemy's head. Before he was killed, Cuchulain strapped himself to a standing stone so that he would die standing up.

Prince Rama

THE WATER TWINS
The Dogon people of Mali in West Africa say that the creator spirit Amma first mated with the Earth, and the Nommo (water) twins were born. Human on the top half and snakelike on the bottom half, the twins were made out of the life-force of Amma. The Nommo were green in color, and clothed their mother Earth with plants and trees. They are believed to make an outline of every newborn soul, giving it a twin nature, both male and female.

HEROIC HERACLES
The Greek hero Heracles (Hercules in Latin) was the son of Zeus by a mortal woman, Alcmene. As an infant he proved his divine descent by strangling two deadly serpents sent by Zeus's jealous wife Hera. Hera's hatred pursued Heracles all his life, robbing him of his destined throne.

The Nommo stand between Earth and sky with their arms outstretched on this Dogon leader's stool

Scary monsters

Giants are found throughout mythology. Their size makes them terrifying, but often they are portrayed as slow, stupid, and easily outwitted, like the Cyclops Polyphemus, who believes that the hero Odysseus's name is Nobody and yells out "Nobody is hurting me" when Odysseus blinds him. Many of the first beings were monsters, such as Ymir, the Norse frost giant.

Cyclopes had only one eye

Fierce incisors tear meat from the bone

ONE-EYED OGRE
Polyphemus was one of the legendary Cyclopes, one-eyed giants with ferocious appetites. He was blinded by Odysseus, who plunged a red-hot stake into his eye. But Polyphemus's father, Poseidon, was so enraged that he persecuted Odysseus — wrecking his ships, drowning his crews, and keeping him from his home for ten long years.

Skulls of mastodons (extinct elephant-like mammals) were once believed to be Cyclopes' skulls

Greedy Cyclopes could devour whole carcasses at one sitting

Tunic made from the hides of the Cyclops's prey

Cyclopes tore their prey limb from limb

Ancestor worship

IN MANY CULTURES, FEAR OF THE EVIL POWER of spirits of the dead is balanced by a belief in the protective power of the spirits of ancestors, who are believed to watch over and guide the living. For this reason offerings may be made to ancestors' shrines. For instance, in China the head of a family must make regular sacrifices of food at the graves of his ancestors; if not, the "hungry ghosts" may cause trouble. In both China and Japan, wooden tablets inscribed with the names of ancestors are kept in a household shrine. The duty that the living owe to the dead was never more pressing than in ancient Egypt, where it was vital that the eldest living son of deceased parents raise a monument to their memory and pronounce their names every time he passed it, to keep their names alive.

ROMULUS AND REMUS
Romulus was the mythical founder of Rome; his name means simply "Roman." The twins Romulus and Remus were the sons of the war god Mars. Abandoned as babies, they were suckled by a wolf and raised by a shepherd. The brothers argued about who should found Rome, and Romulus killed Remus with a spade. But Romulus was soon swept off to heaven by his father, where he became a god and was worshiped by the citizens of Rome.

Bronze Yoruba figurine from Benin, West Africa

Procession of Oshun's devotees

Female figure from Middle Sepik River, Papua New Guinea

OSHUN WORSHIP
Ancestors are worshiped in many parts of Africa and are prayed to for good health, fertility, and good fortune. The Yoruba people of West Africa worship Oshun, goddess of the river that bears the same name. Oshun was married to the thunder god Shango and has human descendants. People bathe in the Oshun River to protect themselves from disease. Women, in particular, consult the goddess Oshun in cases of family problems or illness.

LIFE-GIVING ANCESTORS
In New Guinea, carved figures of ancestors were present at *moguru* (life-giving ceremonies) at which the young were initiated into adulthood and the men gained prowess as fighters. In the Papuan Gulf, the fierce Kerua headhunters hung human skulls from carved boards as offerings to ancestral beings.

COLOSSAL CHIEFS
On Rapa Nui (Easter Island), a remote and barren island of volcanic rock stranded in the eastern Pacific, stand hundreds of monolithic stone figures. They are *moai* – figures of dead chiefs who were regarded as descendants of the gods.

FEAST OF LANTERNS
The *bon* festival, held in Japan each July, is known as the Feast of Lanterns. It is held in honor of the spirits of the dead, which return to Earth for the three days of the festival. Relatives of the deceased pray at shrines, where they leave food and other treats for the spirits to feast on.

DREAMTIME ANCESTORS
The Dreamtime is the eternal present in which the revered ancestors of the Australian Aborigines exist, constantly creating the world. Creation story designs, shown to the Aborigines by the ancestors, are still painted on bodies, rocks, and bark, as in the painting (left) from Arnhem Land, North Australia. Aborigines carve pictures showing events in the Dreamtime on sacred wooden and stone artifacts, called *churinga*. These objects embody ancestral spiritual power and must not be seen by women or the uninitiated.

Aboriginal stone knife similar to those used by the eternal ancestors to create humans

Bark sheath

Papuan ancestral tablet, or ceremonial board

Evil forces

Gap-toothed Louhi as an eagle-woman with scythe-like claws

BESIDES GODS OF DEATH and sterility, there are many demons and forces of evil in world mythology. Balanced against these are forces of good which came into being to rid the world of evil. In Siberia it is told how the creator Ulgan made himself a companion, Erlik, from mud floating on the primal ocean. But Erlik, jealous of Ulgan, saved mud to try to build his own world, and he breathed life into humankind without Ulgan's permission. For these betrayals, Erlik was banished to the underworld, where he sits surrounded by evil spirits. Evil beings are very active in Hindu mythology, which has many antigods and demons. One of the most fearsome of all evil spirits is Vucub-Caquix, the Mayan monster macaw who claimed to be both the sun and the moon. He was killed in a terrible battle by the hero twins Hunahpu and Xbalanque, though not before he had torn off Hunahpu's arm.

WICKED LOUHI
The Finnish hag Louhi promised the smith Ilmarinen her daughter in return for the Sampo — a magic mill that grinds out grain, salt, and money. But Louhi proved treacherous, so Ilmarinen stole back the Sampo and set sail. Louhi turned into a bird and attacked the boat. In the struggle, the Sampo fell to the bottom of the sea, where it still grinds out salt to this day.

TREACHEROUS TRICKSTER
Loki, the Norse trickster god, turned against the other gods and brought about the death of Balder the Beautiful, son of the god Odin. For this, he is bound in agony, with poison dripping onto his face, until the final battle of Ragnarok, when he will lead an army from Hel against the gods in a ship made from dead men's nails.

Vajrapani holds a thunderbolt in his right hand

Tibetan statue of Vajrapani in his "ferocious" form

Fiery headdress encrusted with turquoise

DESTROYER OF EVIL
The Tibetan Vajrapani destroys the wicked with his *vajra* (thunderbolt), which spits lightning. One of eight main bodhisattvas, or Buddhist saints, Vajrapani shares characteristics with Indra, the Hindu god of the skies.

Vajrapani, wielder of the thunderbolt, is a symbol of law and order

Baba Yaga uses her pestle to stir up storms and spread disease

CANNIBAL WITCH
Baba Yaga is the cannibal witch of Russian myth. She lives in a revolving hut supported by hen's feet, and travels through the air in a mortar. Her male equivalent is Koshchei the Deathless, who abducts maidens and can turn into a dragon.

SULKY SUSANO

While bathing, the Japanese god Izanagi gave birth to three powerful divinities: the sun goddess Amaterasu, moon god Tsuki-Yomi, and Susano, the god of storms and chaos. Susano was meant to rule the sea, but he threw a tantrum and said he would rather go to the underworld. He flung a skinned horse into Amaterasu's sacred weaving hall, so was banished to Earth. There he rescued Kusa-nada-hime, the Rice Paddy Princess, from an eight-headed dragon, and made her his wife.

Text from a 19th-century print of the storm god Susano and his wife

Rice Paddy
Princess Kusa-nada-hime

FIRST HUMAN SACRIFICE

When the Aztec goddess Coatlicue was pregnant with the supreme god Huitzilopochtli, she was attacked and murdered by her jealous daughter, Coyolxauhqui, and Coyolxauhqui's 400 brothers. But Huitzilopochtli leaped fully formed from his mother's decapitated body and slew his sister, making her the first human sacrifice.

Each of Durga's ten hands holds a special weapon — a symbol of divine power

INVINCIBLE DURGA

The Hindu warrior goddess Durga was one of the guises of the great goddess Devi. Durga was created to fight the *asuras* (demon enemies of the gods), who had conquered heaven. In each of her ten hands Durga holds a special weapon that she used to cut off the head of the buffalo-king of the *asuras*.

Susano, the
Japanese storm god

Superheroes

MEN AND WOMEN WHO PERFORM great feats of daring and courage are celebrated in all mythologies. Often, they are said to be the children of gods or to be specially favored by the gods. Some heroes can defeat a whole series of enemies in single combat and rid countries of the monsters that plague them. Others, such as Hiawatha, are celebrated as peacemakers rather than as warriors. A typical hero is the Tibetan Gesar, who was a god chosen to be born as a man to rid the world of demons. Gesar became a powerful warrior king, with an immortal horse that flew through the sky and spoke all languages. At the end of his life, Gesar retired to heaven, but one day he will return, for evil can never be wholly defeated.

Polynices's corpse is left to rot

BRAVE ANTIGONE
Antigone was the daughter of Oedipus, king of Thebes in Greece. After his death, his two sons, Eteocles and Polynices, fought over the throne and killed each other. Their uncle Creon buried Eteocles with honor but threw the body of Polynices out to rot, regarding him as a traitor. Although threatened with death, Antigone bravely defied her uncle and gave Polynices a token burial, sprinkling three handfuls of dust over the corpse. Creon then walled her up in a cave without food or water, so she hanged herself.

When Krishna plays his magic flute, women within earshot join him to dance

Krishna is always blue, which shows that he is an incarnation of Vishnu

Krishna stands on a lotus flower, symbol of the earth

North American Indians made wampum (bead) belts to mark peace agreements

Beads are made from white and purple clam shells

PEACEMAKER
Dekanah-wida was born to bring tidings of peace from the chief of the Sky Spirits to five warring Native American Indian tribes. Dekanah-wida made the Mohawk chief, Hiawatha, his peacemaker. Hiawatha then traveled between the tribes, persuading them to form the Iroquois League, whose members swore to live in peace together.

DEMON DODGER
Krishna is the eighth avatar (incarnation) of the Hindu god Vishnu and is worshiped as a god in his own right. When he was a child, his mother took him to the countryside to escape the demon king Kansa, who was persecuting them. Kansa sent a female demon to poison him, but Krishna sucked the life out of her instead.

Sigurd kills the dragon

Fafnir the dragon

DRAGON SLAYER
The Scandinavian hero Sigurd slew the dragon Fafnir so that he could claim its treasure. Sigurd had been urged to kill the dragon by Regin, Fafnir's brother, who asked Sigurd to return with the dragon's heart. But Regin was plotting to kill Sigurd and steal the treasure for himself. Some birds tried to warn Sigurd, but he could not understand them. Fortunately, as he cooked the dragon's heart he burned his thumb and, putting it in his mouth, tasted the dragon's blood. The blood enabled Sigurd to understand the birds. Learning that Regin meant to betray him, Sigurd killed him and kept the treasure.

When Yi shot the suns, they fell to the Earth in the shape of crows

The Minotaur had a bull's head on a man's body

MONSTER KILLER
Theseus was the greatest of all Athenian heroes, said to be the son of the sea god Poseidon. His most famous feat was to slay the ferocious Minotaur. King Minos of Crete regularly fed the Minotaur with children from Athens; Theseus volunteered himself to be fed to the Minotaur and, with the help of Minos's daughter Ariadne, killed the Minotaur in the labyrinth (maze) in which he lived.

Yi won a potion of immortality, but Chang E drank it herself and floated to the moon

Heavenly gates are guarded by two soldiers

YI THE ARCHER
The Chinese say that originally there were ten suns, the sons of the emperor of the eastern heavens. The suns took turns lighting the sky. But once, all ten went out to play. Together they were so hot that they began to scorch the Earth, so the emperor sent Yi, the heavenly archer, to teach them a lesson. Yi shot down nine of them. The emperor was so upset that he stripped Yi and his wife, Chang E, of their immortality and banished them from heaven.

Mortals on their way to heaven to become immortals

Perseus holds Medusa's severed head

GREEK GUARDIAN
Perseus was the son of the Greek god Zeus and the maiden Danaë. To save his mother from an unwanted marriage, Perseus agreed to fetch the head of the Gorgon Medusa, whose glance turned the onlooker to stone. Using a bronze shield as a mirror so that he did not have to meet the Gorgon's gaze, Perseus cut off her head. He then used the head to turn his mother's unwelcome suitor to stone.

Kneeling men and women mourn for the dead

Gilgamesh clutches a captured lion cub

Altars full of food

KING GILGAMESH
Gilgamesh was the great hero of ancient Mesopotamia. He was a semidivine king, who fought monsters with his friend Enkidu. When Gilgamesh scorned the love of the goddess Ishtar, she sent a great bull to destroy him, but Gilgamesh and Enkidu slew the bull.

Scenes of the underworld

Chinese funeral banner, 2nd century B.C.

Medusa lies dead at Perseus's feet

Divine weapons

SWORD, SPEAR, AX, OR BOW, the weapons of the gods often mirror those of humans. The Norse all-father Odin, for instance, had a magical spear that he used to stir up war. But the gods can also unleash natural forces as weapons, most notably the thunderbolt (lightning), which has been a weapon of sky gods all over the world. Weapons could be improvised out of anything: the club of the semi-divine Greek hero Heracles was simply an uprooted olive tree. The Navajo hero twins were given bows with arrows of lightning by their father, the Sun god, to help them rid the world of monsters. Even when caught without their weapons, gods can punish the insolent or wicked. When the Greek hunter Actaeon spied the goddess Artemis bathing, without her bow and arrows, she turned him into a stag and let his own hounds maul him to death.

The Greek god Zeus wields a thunderbolt

BATTLING BROTHERS
This 19th-century chief's ax is a symbol of Tane, the Oceanic god of the forests, who was himself shaped by craftsmen with axes. After Tane separated Earth and sky, he and his brother Tangaroa, god of the seas, began a fierce battle. Tangaroa lashed the land with his waves, trying to wash it away. Tane supplied men with canoes, spears, fishhooks, and nets to catch Tangaroa's fish. Craftsmen pray to Tane to put their axes to sleep at night, and to wake them up in the morning.

Shango looks both ways, so that no one can escape him

THUNDER AND LIGHTNING
The terrifying energy of an electrical storm has been interpreted by many people as the anger of the gods. Thunderbolts have been used as weapons by many gods, including the Olympian Zeus. Native Americans revere the Thunderbird, which produces thunder by flapping its wings, and lightning by flashing its eyes. Tupan, an Amazonian thunder god, caused thunder and lightning by crossing the sky in a dugout canoe.

SPITTER OF THUNDERBOLTS
Ceremonial staffs such as this symbolize Shango, thunder god of the Yoruba people of West Africa. His symbol is the double ax, which represents thunderbolts. Shango was originally a king and was given the power to spit thunderbolts by the trickster god Eshu. Being hit by lightning is thought to be a sign of Shango's anger.

To terrify Shango's enemies, his devotees hold thunderbolt staffs as they dance to loud drumbeats

MAGICAL SWORD
The Norse god Frey had a sword that would fight on its own. But he gave the sword to Skirnir, his servant, as a reward for winning him the hand of the beautiful maiden Gerd. It is said that at the final battle of Ragnarok, Frey will fight the fire giant Surt, who has a blade that flames like the sun. But without his sword, Frey will be defeated, allowing Surt to burn up the world.

Iron sword from Denmark

ANCESTRAL WEAPON

The boomerang was an important weapon of the Australian Aborigines. The first boomerang represented the Aboriginal Rainbow Snake, and is said to have been made from the tree between heaven and Earth. A myth of the Binbinga tribe of Australia tells how the ancestral snake Bobbi-Bobbi made the first boomerang from one of his ribs.

Rainbow Snake

Aboriginal war boomerangs are designed to fly in straight lines and travel great distances

17th-century brass *vajras* from Tibet representing thunderbolts

Tibetans use vajras, *believed to hold magical powers, in rituals and while meditating*

BLADE OF IRON

Ogun is the god of iron and war among the Yoruba people of West Africa. When the Earth was still a watery waste, Ogun used to climb down from heaven on a spider's web to hunt in the marshland. After the Earth was formed, Ogun cleared the land with his iron blade. He was last seen sinking into the ground with his sword.

Ritual sword used in Ogun worship

Ceremonial bow and arrows

GODDESS OF HUNTING

Diana is the Roman name for the Greek goddess of hunting and archery, Artemis. Although Diana was the goddess of the hunt, she was also the protector of all wild animals.

Vows taken in the name of Ogun, with the tongue on a blade or some other iron object, are completely binding

Diana, protector of wild animals

Silver replica of Thor's hammer from Denmark

Thor in his chariot pulled by goats

THOR'S LUCKY HAMMER

The Norse thunder god Thor was the son of the all-father Odin; his mother was the Earth. He had a wonderful hammer, *Mjollnir*, which never missed its target, and returned to his hand when thrown. Vikings wore pendants in the shape of Thor's hammer for protection. Large replicas of these lucky hammers were also used to bless weddings, births, and funerals.

Gods of war

HUMAN HISTORY HAS BEEN SHAPED by war and conflict, and gods of war have a high status in many mythologies. The Greeks had two war gods: Ares, who was the god of fighting; and Athena, who was the goddess of strategy. That a goddess should take an interest in warfare is not unusual. Ishtar was the Mesopotamian goddess of both love and war; the Irish had a triple war goddess, the Morrigan, who could change into a crow and settled in that form on the shoulder of the dying hero Cuchulain. But most war gods are male, and many of them, like Ares and Odin, are bloodthirsty, reveling in slaughter.

GREEK GODDESS OF STRATEGY
While Ares was the Greek god of fighting, Athena was the goddess of strategy and wisdom. She sprang from the head of her father Zeus, fully armed and ready for battle. Athena is always depicted in full armor, with the head of the Gorgon Medusa fixed to her breastplate.

The divine blacksmith Gu taught the first humans how to make tools so that they could work the land

Mars wears a warrior's helmet

PROTECTIVE MARS
Mars was the Roman god of war. He seems to have been originally a god of agriculture, and even as a war god he retained a protective function, unlike his brutal and violent Greek equivalent, Ares. He was one of the most important Roman gods and was believed to have fathered Romulus, the founder of Rome. Soldiers made sacrifices to Mars before and after battle.

GOD OF IRON
Gu was the fifth-born child of Mawu-Lisa, the West African creator god. Mawu gave her strength to Gu. He is made of iron and is sometimes depicted as an iron sword. In this form, Mawu-Lisa used him to clear the Earth for humans to live in. Gu is the god of iron and consequently of war, since war is waged with iron weapons.

Iron statue of Gu, war god of the Fon people of West Africa

WARRING KU
Ku was the war god of Hawaii. He had many names descriptive of his various roles. As patron of woodworkers he was Ku-adzing-out-the-canoe. When the gods were trapped between their parents Earth and sky, Ku-of-the-angry-face wanted to kill them, but the other gods fought Ku. This was the beginning of warfare.

FIGHTING SPIRITS

The Valkyries of the Norse god Odin were female spirits who rode to battle to give victory or death, according to Odin's will. They also waited on the souls of dead warriors in the hall of Valhalla. The name Valkyrie means "chooser of the slain." The Norse fertility goddess Freya was said to ride to battle and claim half the slain.

Valkyries rode horses to fetch dead warriors from the battlefield and take them to Odin's Valhalla

All-father Odin wears an elaborate winged helmet

Chinese bronze sword, 4th century B.C.

NORSE WAR GODS

The Viking gods were among the most warlike of all. Their leader, Odin (left), was the god of battle, inspiring his warriors with a fighting frenzy. Only those who died in battle joined him in Valhalla after death.

Spears were among Norse warriors' most prized possessions

DEMON KILLER

Skanda, the six-headed Hindu god of war, is the son of Shiva. He was born to kill the demon Taraka, who had been oppressing the gods. Skanda rides a peacock, on which he traveled around the world in a contest of learning with his brother Ganesh. Ganesh, who stayed at home and read, knew more than Skanda when he returned.

CHINESE WARRIOR GOD

Guan Di is the Chinese god of war. Originally a humble seller of bean curd, he devoted himself to study, and he is still regarded as a patron of literature. However, after he killed a magistrate, he had to flee his home and fend for himself. Guan Di became a soldier, one of the three famous Brothers of the Peach Orchard, and, in 1594 A.D., was elevated to the status of god of war.

Statue of Guan Di, the Chinese god of war

Contacting the spirits

ANCIENT GREEKS TOOK THEIR PROBLEMS to the oracle of Apollo at Delphi, where a priestess, called the Pythia (Pythoness), went into a trance and uttered strange words that were then interpreted by a priest. Among the Vikings, *volvas* (prophetesses) answered questions in a similar way. Siberian shamans, Native American medicine men, and Aboriginal men of high degree all use drumming, dance, and song to enter an altered mental state in which they can communicate with the spirit world. Offerings and sacrifices may also bridge the gap between the two worlds, as when worshipers are possessed by the gods in Voodoo rites. Among the Yoruba of West Africa, the god of fate, Eshu, uses sacrifices to plead with the other gods, or to appease evil spirits on behalf of humanity.

GUIDING GOD
The Greek god Hermes (Mercury in Rome) was the messenger of the gods, and also the guide of souls into the underworld. As he was always going to and fro, he became the protector of all travelers.

Pipe of carved human bone

Priest speaks into this hole to distort his voice and make it boom out

VOICE DISGUISER
A priest of the Tiv people of Nigeria would use this voice disguiser to allow the ancestor god Tiv to speak through him in a piercing cry.

Half-halo represents Ganesh's divinity

Noose to trap delusion

Jizo, the protector of children and travelers

CONVEYOR OF PRAYERS
Ganesh, the wise elephant-headed son of Shiva, is the god of all good enterprises. Hindus ask Ganesh to pass on their requests to Shiva. They make offerings to the potbellied god before going on a journey, starting a business, or making plans for a wedding.

GOOD-LUCK CHARMS
Japanese *fuda,* or amulets, bear the name of a god and are used to ward off evil and misfortune and to bring good luck. They are often placed on household shrines to protect the family.

豊川閣窪嶺守護攸

建長寺

The ancestors sit in the top branches of the world tree; the shaman climbs up to ask for their help

Shamans' spirit helpers often take animal form

Drumbeats are used to call the spirits that will help the shaman

Metal ornaments hanging from the belt protect against evil spirits

THE SHAMAN
A shaman is someone who has had a life-changing vision that enables him or her to enter a trance and fly to the spirit world. A shaman's power is usually used for healing, though it can also cause disease or death.

Souls of the unborn nest in the tree

Dancers hang from rawhide thongs sewn through the skin

SUN DANCE
In rituals such as the Sun Dance, Plains Native Americans underwent excruciating physical tortures as sacrifices to the Great Spirit. Once they had fulfilled their vows, dancers hoped to receive a vision.

The pipe bowl is round, like the world, and outside it is the endless universe

PIPES OF PEACE
The sacred pipe is an important part of many Native American rituals, bringing peace and healing. Tobacco was believed to have the power to summon good spirits, ward off evil ones, and bring either good luck or bad. Communal smoking helped to reinforce the ties between families, tribes, and the universe.

Tiger spirits often teach shamans their craft

Spirits

The world tree houses all souls

Siberian shaman's outfit

38457

Love, fortune, and happiness

MANY PEOPLE WORSHIP deities who will bring them luck in life. In ancient times, for instance, the Romans had a cult of the goddess Fortuna (good luck). The Ewe people of Togo in West Africa believe that the soul of each unborn child must first visit Ngolimeno, the "Mother of the Spirit People." If they please her, she will grant them a happy life. The Japanese worship seven gods of luck, of whom one, Benten, is a goddess. But it is the Chinese who have outdone all others in the worship of fortune and happiness. The lucky Ho-Ho twins (right) are often shown attending Tsai Shen, the god of wealth. Another common trio is Fu Shen, god of happiness; Lu Shen, god of good luck; and Shou Shen, god of longevity.

THE WINGED GOD
Cupid (Eros in Greek) was the mischievous Roman god of love, often shown as a cheeky infant with a bow and arrows. Some of his arrows had gold tips and caused people to fall in love; others were tipped with lead and had the opposite effect.

Venus of Rome rises from the ocean on a scallop shell

BORN OF FOAM
The Greek goddess of love and desire, Aphrodite (Venus to the Romans), was born from the foam of the sea. She devoted herself to pleasure, prided herself on never doing any work, and was often assisted by Eros (Cupid to the Romans). Aphrodite was married to the smith god Hephaestus but had many lovers among both gods and men. As Venus she was the mother of the Roman hero Aeneas.

Each twin carries a jar containing a lotus of purity and perfection

Statue depicting the birth of Aphrodite, Greek goddess of love

Terracotta figure of Aphrodite made in the 2nd century B.C.E

The gods are standing on beds of lotus flowers

The head of each twin is decorated with a lotus

GOOD FORTUNE GODS
The Seven Gods of Luck (Shichi Fukujin) are Bishamon, Daikoku, Ebisu, Fukurokuju, Hotei, Jorojin, and the goddess Benten – the bringer of love, happiness, and good fortune. The Shichi Fukujin are often shown together on their treasure ship. Their treasures include a hat of invisibility, a lucky rain hat, keys to the divine treasure house, a purse that never empties, a cloak of feathers, rolls of silk, and scrolls or books.

Benten rides an ox, symbol of good fortune

These Ho-Ho gods symbolize happy relations between couples

CONFUSED DEITY
Kwan-non is the god or goddess of mercy in Japanese Buddhism. Priests regard Kwan-non as a male divinity, but most people pray to him as a goddess, and he appears in 33 female forms. This statue shows her (or him) holding a baby. Expectant mothers would pray to this statue as Koyasu Kwan-non ("Kwan-non of easy childbirth").

Love medicines are inserted into pockets on the chest of each doll

LOVE DOLLS
These Native American medicine dolls are used by the Menominee of the western Great Lakes to ensure that a husband and wife remain faithful to each other. The male doll is named after the husband and the female after the wife, and the two are tied together face to face. The Pottawatomi, also of the western Great Lakes, used dolls as charms to make one person fall in love with another.

HO-HO TWINS
The two immortals called Ho are the patrons of Chinese merchants. Besides bringing prosperity, they represent harmonious union between couples, because the word "ho" means harmony. Their names were originally Han Shan and Shih-teh. Han Shan was a holy fool who attached himself to the monastery at Kuo-ching Ssu; the monks rejected him, but Shih-teh, an orphan in the kitchens, saved scraps to feed him.

Tricksters

LIGHTHEARTED COMEDY and dark humor are introduced into myths by trickster figures, such as the Native American Coyote (left), whose insatiable curiosity and love of mischief leave havoc and confusion in their wake. Tricksters may be animal, human, or both. Some tricksters hover between good and evil, as does the cunning Norse god Loki. The Ashanti people of West Africa tell tales of Anansi, the cunning spider-man, who won the famous stories of the sky god Nyame. By a series of clever tricks, Anansi trapped all the creatures that Nyame thought were impossible to catch. For instance, he caught the fairy Mmoatia by making a tar baby, to which Mmoatia stuck fast. When Anansi delivered the creatures to Nyame, he was so impressed that he willingly gave Anansi the stories. Since then, the tales have been called spider stories.

WILY COYOTE
Many Native American peoples tell stories of the wily Coyote, who both tricks and is tricked. Coyote has many human characteristics — he is greedy and selfish, and his exploits lead to bad as well as good consequences.

Cowrie shells are used by Eshu to predict the future

MISCHIEVOUS ESHU
Eshu is the trickster god of the Yoruba people of West Africa. His many guises include giant, dwarf, rude boy, wise old man, and a priest, as seen here. Eshu loves mischief. For instance, he broke up a firm friendship between two men by wearing a hat that was white on one side but black on the other, causing them to quarrel about the color of his hat.

Eshu holds a small statue of himself

Mask worn to impersonate Hare

Hare climbs up the mask

CUNNING HARE
Hare is an African animal trickster who became known in America as Brer Rabbit. Cunning and wily, Hare always outwits the other animals, except when Tortoise challenged him to a race. Instead of running, Tortoise placed members of his family all around the course and sat waiting for Hare at the finish line.

Figures represent Eshu in his various guises

An Eshu priest would wear this statue by hooking the headdress over his shoulder, just as Eshu is doing with the statue he is holding

SUN CATCHER
Maui-of-a-thousand-tricks is the trickster hero of Polynesian mythology. He fished up the islands with his magic hook, pushed up the heavens, stole fire for humankind, and snared the sun with his sister's hair to slow it down, so that we have long summer days.

Medicine calabashes (bowls) represent Eshu's magical powers

Tengu rescue the hero Tametomo from the jaws of a giant fish

INVISIBLE TRICKSTERS
The Tengu are Japanese trickster spirits, part-bird, part-man. They are said to be descended from the storm god Susano, who himself got into trouble by playing tricks. Tengu have magic cloaks of invisibility.

GRIMACING GOD
Bes was a popular Egyptian god of music, dance, and laughter, whose grimacing face and comical antics were thought to frighten away evil spirits. He was the protector of mothers in childbirth and the companion of young children. He is always shown sticking his tongue out at the world.

Bacchus's long flowing hair shows his eternal youth

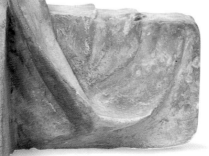

The fish represents the islands that Maui fished up from the sea

INDULGENT GOD
Bacchus (Dionysus in Greek) was the Roman god of wine and ecstasy. His followers were wild women called the Maenads (frenzied ones). When sailors captured Bacchus, his tricks sent them diving madly into the sea, where they turned into dolphins. It was Bacchus who gave King Midas the double-edged gift of turning all that he touched into gold.

Animal idols

GODS AND SPIRITS MAY BE SHOWN in animal form, or as half-human, half-beast. Trickster figures, such as the African spider-man Anansi, may be a man, an animal, or a mixture of both at different times in the same story. Some gods have an animal helper, such as the fox that lived with the Japanese rice god Inari and acted as his messenger. Some gods can transform themselves into animals; the Greek god Zeus, for example, became a bull and then a swan while pursuing his love affairs. Some gods have an animal double, as with the Aztec god Quetzalcoatl and his twin Xolotl — the dog who helped retrieve the bones of humankind from the underworld.

THE BULL OF HEAVEN
This winged bull stood guard over a royal palace in Assyria. The bull was a cult animal all over ancient west Asia. For instance, a bull of heaven was sent to destroy the Sumerian hero Gilgamesh. But Gilgamesh and his friend slew the bull and gave its heart to the sun god Shamash.

Celtic drinking horns tipped with sheeps' heads

THE HORNED ONE
Gods with animals' horns are found in many mythologies. One of the most famous was the Celtic horned god Cernunnos, who was lord of the beasts, and a god of fertility. The goat's horns of the Greek god Pan inspired pictures of the Christian Devil.

Nagas have both protective and destructive powers

Half-human, half-beast

The gods of many peoples are often depicted as half-human, half-animal. This is especially true of the Egyptian gods, nearly all of whom have at least one animal form. For instance, the cow goddess Hathor was also worshipped as the lioness Sekhmet, and the cat Bastet. The dog or jackal god Anubis could also become a snake or a falcon. The Sun god Ra turned himself into a cat to cut off the head of the evil snake Apep that attacked him every night.

19th-century Sri Lankan mask

Fierce face wards off the evil spirits thought to cause sickness

THE SNAKE DEMON
This mask of Naga Rassa, or snake demon, is worn in dances to drive away evil spirits. The nagas (sacred snakes) were descended from the ancient sage Kasyapa, the father of life. Buddhists tell how Mucilinda, a king of the nagas, grew more heads to shelter the Buddha from a storm.

SEKHMET
The Sun god Ra sent the raging lioness Sekhmet to destroy humankind. But when Ra changed his mind, the only way to stop Sekhmet from killing was to make her drunk.

SOBEK
The Egyptian crocodile god Sobek, son of the creator goddess Neith, was the ever-hungry lord of the waters in the Nile River. He was depicted as a crocodile or as a man with a crocodile's head. As Sobek-Ra, he was an aspect of the Sun god.

ANUBIS
The jackal-headed god Anubis made the first mummy when he wrapped the body parts of the god Osiris in cloth to put them back together. In the underworld, Anubis weighed the hearts of the dead against the feather of justice.

When Garuda soars into the sky, he symbolizes the human spirit

Golden Garuda's body shines as bright as the Sun — some say he was the Sun in the form of a bird

Vishnu and his wife, Lakshmi, ride on Garuda

Eagle-like wings

Garuda has the body of a human

Legs are covered with golden feathers

Clawed feet enabled Garuda to pick up the snakes that he devoured

KING OF THE BIRDS
Half-human, half-bird, Garuda was the Hindu king of the birds and destroyer of evil. He was ridden by the great god Vishnu. Garuda was the son of Kasyapa (left). But Garuda hated his father's other offspring, the nagas, because their mother made his mother, Vinata, a slave in the underworld. To save her, Garuda had to steal a cup of the elixir of immortality from the gods.

Brass figure of Garuda from Tibet

Mythical beasts

Stories about mythical creatures are found all over the world. Native Americans say that many monsters peopled the world at the beginning of time, until great heroes defeated them. Some people believe that mythical beasts are based on garbled accounts of real creatures — that unicorns, for instance, are really rhinoceroses. But mythical creatures seem to be more a focus for fear, awe, and wonder than simply mistaken natural history. Monsters are sometimes combinations of various animals, such as the griffin, which was half-eagle, half-lion. Just giving an ordinary animal a special feature, such as the ability of the Greek horse Pegasus to fly, transports it from the ordinary world to a realm of wonder.

WILD HORSES
Half-man, half-horse, the centaur was a wild and savage creature. One exception was Chiron, a wise centaur, who was tutor to many Greek heroes. He died after being accidentally wounded by Heracles with a poisoned arrow.

CREATURES OF THE DEEP
In the past, sailors returned from their travels with strange beasts, which they claimed to have fished from the sea. The creature "Jenny Haniver" (above) is actually a dried skate fish. Some of these curious creatures were created by joining the bodies of different animals together. For instance, a monkey's body was grafted onto the tail of a fish to create a merman.

Spiky claws protrude from the dragon's wings

BLOWING HOT AIR
Fire-breathing, winged dragons, who jealously guard their hoards of treasure, feature in many European myths. For instance, the Scandinavian dragon Fafnir was actually a man who turned into a dragon to protect his treasure. Many stories tell of dragon-slaying heroes who rescue maidens or win their hands in marriage. One such hero was Tristan, the Celtic hero who killed a dragon to win the hand of Isolde. Unlike the fearsome European dragon, Chinese dragons are kindly and serpentlike.

Dragons breathe fire through their mouths

Unicorn horns were prized for their supposed ability to detect poison

HORN OF PURITY
The unicorn was a white horselike creature, with a single spiral horn growing from its forehead. It was said that if a unicorn dipped its horn into water, the water would become pure. In fact, the unicorn was such a powerful symbol of purity that supposed unicorn horns (actually the tusks of narwhal whales) once sold for 20 times their weight in gold; one was even said to be worth a city.

DREADFUL LOCKS
Medusa was one of the three Gorgons — hideous creatures with snakes for hair. Anyone who looked at her would be turned to stone. But the Greek hero Perseus killed Medusa by looking at her reflection in a bronze shield as he cut off her head.

Medusa's hair was made of writhing snakes

WINGS OF A HERO
The winged horse Pegasus was ridden by the Greek hero Bellerophon. When his enemies ordered Bellerophon to kill the monstrous Chimera (below), they hoped he would die in the attempt. Instead, however, riding Pegasus, Bellerophon swooped down on the monster from above and riddled it with arrows.

Pegasus was born from Medusa's blood

A serpent formed the Chimera's tail

The middle part of the Chimera was a she-goat

European dragons have batlike wings

Thorny hooks protrude from the dragon's tail

HEADS AND TAILS
The Chimera was a fire-breathing monster made up of the body parts of various animals. It was one of the children of the half-nymph, half-serpent Echidna, who also spawned such monsters as the Sphinx and the 100-headed serpent Ladon. The Chimera was slain by the Greek hero Bellerophon.

The Chimera had the forequarters of a lion

The dragon's skin is covered in scales like those of a serpent or fish

Clawed feet are seen on both Chinese and European dragons

Painting the story

BEATING THE DRUM
Across Africa, drums are used to beat out rhythms to accompany reenactment rituals and dances. A drum is thought to have a spirit living in it, which may possess those who dance to its beat. The *bata* drum, used by the Yoruba tribe of West Africa in ceremonies to honor the thunder god Shango, is said to have been made by Shango to frighten his enemies.

THERE ARE MANY WAYS OF TELLING stories other than through speech, and many myths are "told" through ritual, dance, or art rather than through narrative storytelling. In the chantways (right) of the Native American Navajo, sand painting, song, prayer, dance, and ritual combine to relive complex myths, which are remembered not for their story content but for their healing spiritual power. The Australian Aboriginal stories of the Dreamtime are recalled not just in words and ceremonies but also through traditional designs painted on the body. The same designs are used in bark paintings and the ground paintings of central Australia, which are very similar to Navajo sand paintings.

Wooden snake stick (symbol of lightning)

The headdress varies in size and design, according to the character

Noble characters paint their faces green

Heroes wear red jackets

STORIES THROUGH DANCE
Kathakali dancers enact stories from the two great epics of India, the Mahabharata and the Ramayana. The essence of both stories is the eternal struggle between good and evil, and dances usually end with the conquering of a demon by a hero.

SNAKE DANCE
Native Americans held rituals to ensure rain and good crops. In the Hopi snake dance, dancers hold live snakes in their mouths. Snake sticks are set up in ceremonial chambers. After the dance, the snakes are released to take the dancers' prayers to the gods.

Beats of the double-sided drum call up new creations

Ankle bracelets

The skirt is made up of many layers of white cotton

RING OF FLAMES
The Hindu god Siva dances the tandava, which represents the creation and destruction of the world. He dances in a circle of flames — one hand cupping the flame of destruction, the other holding the drum of creation. As he dances, Siva tramples the dwarf of ignorance beneath his feet.

Mudstone

Sandstone

Gypsum

Chalk

Brown pigment

Yellow pigment

Red pigment

Charcoal

Sacred sandpainting

The sand paintings of the Native American Navajo are temporary altars created and destroyed as part of healing rituals known as chantways. Their Navajo name means "place where the gods come and go." Each painting must be re-created in exactly the same way each time, or the ritual will not work.

Only men can become qualified sand painters

Pigments are trickled onto the sand through the thumb and forefinger

The Oculate Being has bulging eyes

POWDER PAINTS
Sand painting pigments are gathered by the family sponsoring the ceremony and ground in a mortar and pestle. Pigments include sandstone, mudstone, charcoal from hard oak, cornmeal, powdered flower petals, and plant pollen.

CHANTWAY CEREMONIES
Sand paintings are made by skilled painters under the direction of the singer who is in charge of the ritual. An average sand painting takes six men about four hours to complete. When the painting is finished, the singer sprinkles it with protective pollen and says a prayer; then the ritual begins.

POWERFUL PICTURES
Sand paintings contain exact depictions of the Navajo " holy people" — supernatural beings whose powers are evoked in the chantway ceremonies. Such sand paintings are sacred and powerful. This nonsacred sand painting, made for commercial sale, shows a typical holy person.

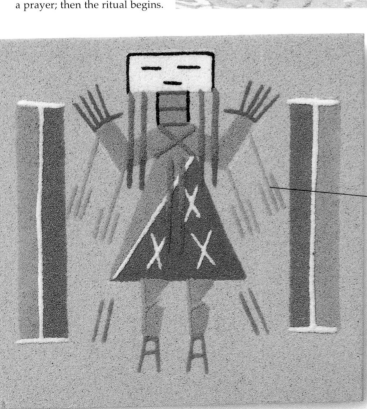

Bracelets and armlets hang from the wrists and elbows

Snake-like tongue

WOVEN STORY
This woven textile from the Paracas people of Peru is full of the spirits and demons of Paracas mythology, including bug-eyed Oculate Beings, shown as heads with no bodies and long tongues snaking out between prominent teeth.

Alpaca wool weaving from southern Peru, 600–200 B.C.

Universal creatures

MANY COMMON THEMES run through world mythology. One theme connects human beings with other animals — we are descended from them, or they are our reincarnated ancestors, or they represent gods or spirits whom we must worship or appease. In many creation myths, such as the stories of the Aboriginal Dreamtime, the first inhabitants of the world are neither animal nor human but a mixture of both. This is true of many "animal" gods, such as the African spider-man Anansi. The Egyptian gods all have one or more animal forms as well as human forms; even in the Judeo-Christian tradition the devil can take the form of a snake.

TURTLE WORLD
Many Native American peoples believe that the Earth is supported on the back of a turtle — a belief that is also found in Hindu mythology. The creator god Brahma took the shape of a turtle to create the world. Vishnu became a turtle to help the gods win the elixir of immortality. In North America and in Africa the turtle is also a trickster figure.

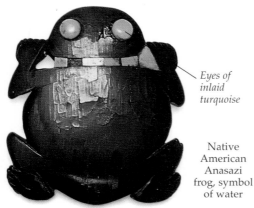

Eyes of inlaid turquoise

Native American Anasazi frog, symbol of water

THE FROG
A West African story telling how Frog brought death into the world is echoed by a Native American myth which says that Frog was so angry with his Maker that he spat poison into the Maker's water, killing him and all his creatures. To the Maori of New Zealand, the frog was a rain god, an association also made by Native Americans. In Egypt Heket was a frog goddess of childbirth and resurrection.

Recurring crocodiles

Because of their fearsome appearance, crocodiles appear in many myths. Often they are threatening creatures — for instance the Basuto tribe of Africa believes that a crocodile can seize a man's shadow and pull him under water. But on the island of Sulawesi, in Indonesia, crocodiles are addressed as "grandfather" because they may be an ancestor. And it is believed that a crocodile will attack a human only when told to do so by the god Poe Mpalaburu.

Detail from a Papuan shield

Man inside the belly of a crocodile

FATHER CROCODILE
Papuans believe that crocodiles have magical powers. One myth of the Kiwai Papuans tells how the creator, Ipila, carved the first four humans from wood and gave them sago to eat. But two of them began to eat meat and turned into crocodile-men. The clans descended from them claim the crocodile as their father.

Turquoise mosaic squares

Coral pieces add color to the nose and mouth

Ceremonial snake pendant worn by priests of the Aztec rain god Tlaloc

LIFE-GIVING SERPENT
The snake is probably the most widely revered creature in world mythology. It is often associated with the primal waters from which all life was created. In the Americas, the double-headed serpent is associated with life-giving rain. Australian Aborigines credit the creation of the landscape to the Rainbow Snake, the source of shamanic power. The Rainbow Snake Aido-Hwedo arches over the sky and under the sea in West Africa.

Egyptian crocodile god Sobek

Mayan crocodile incense burner

HEAVENLY MONSTER
In Mayan art there are numerous depictions of the celestial, or cosmic, monster, a being with a crocodile's body and two heads, one at the front and one at the back. The monster is sometimes shown arching over the heavens, its body in the form of clouds.

The crocodile has large, snapping jaws with very sharp teeth

Clawed feet

Golden crocodile figure made by the Ashanti people of West Africa

Dry, scaly skin prevents water loss in the hot African sun

Back feet are webbed

Powerful, whiplike tail

Nile crocodiles are found on riverbanks throughout tropical Africa

AFRICAN ANCESTORS
Many Africans believe crocodiles to be reincarnated people. In West Africa it is said that a person who kills a crocodile will become one. And if someone is attacked by a crocodile, it is believed that the victim must have harmed the crocodile during its human life.

RAVENOUS SOBEK
Ancient Egyptians worshipped crocodiles in the form of the crocodile god Sobek, who was often depicted with the head of a crocodile and the body of a human. Sobek was so hungry that when the dismembered body of Osiris was thrown into the Nile, he ate some of it. The other gods cut out Sobek's tongue for this wicked act.

Death and the underworld

SINCE HUMANITY BEGAN, PEOPLE HAVE told stories to explain what happens after death. The Mayan hero twins Hunahpu and Xbalanque descended to Xibalba, the "place of fright," to rescue their father from One Death, lord of the underworld. The twins survived ordeals in the houses of lances, fire, and jaguars. They then boasted that they had power over death, and to prove it let themselves be killed and ground like flour. When they came back to life, the lords of death were so impressed that they asked to be killed too. But the twins did not revive them, and so the power of death was lessened forever. In his top hat and dark glasses, the Haitian voodoo god Ghede guards the eternal crossroads where the souls of the dead pass their way to the underworld.

The skeleton is commonly used as an image of death

CHINESE JUDGE OF THE DEAD
Yen-lo is the terrifying ruler and judge of the dead in China. First, the souls are weighed: the virtuous are light, the sinful heavy. Then the souls must pass a number of tests and challenges. They are assaulted by demons, attacked by dogs, then allowed one last glimpse of home and family before being given a drink that wipes away all memories. Finally, each soul is reincarnated.

DYING FOR DISOBEDIENCE
The elaborate funeral rites of the Dogon people of West Africa involve dancing and chanting in a secret language. These rituals recount a myth that describes how death entered the world because of the disobedience of young men. Africans do not see death as a final end but believe that the spirits of the dead have power over the living.

Osiris, god of the underworld

Horus, son of Osiris

THE AFTERLIFE
The ancient Egyptians believed that their souls would be weighed against the feather of truth, and that they would then be led into the Hall of the Two Truths to face the lord of the dead, Osiris. The virtuous hoped for a new life in the Field of Reeds, a perfected version of Egypt.

Skirts are red to represent death

AZTEC LORD OF THE UNDERWORLD

Mictlantecuhtli, the Aztec god of death, is usually depicted as a white skeleton spotted with blood. On their way to his peaceful underworld (Mictlan), the dead were reduced to skeletons by a wind of knives. Mictlantecuhtli was said to be the father of Quetzalcoatl, the lord of life.

DAY OF THE DEAD

The Mexican Day of the Dead (November 1) is an occasion for great festivities. Every family prays to the souls of dead relatives so that they will return to Earth for one night. Altars in homes and cemeteries are decorated with food, flowers, and ghoulish sugar models. A candle is lit for each soul to help it find its way back to the land of the living. Many other cultures celebrate a day of the dead, including the Chinese, where it is known as the Feast of the Hungry Ghosts.

The grinning Mictlantecuhtli welcomes the dead to his underworld

Altar skulls are made from sugar and water and are decorated with sugar icing

Souls of the dead are tormented by demons in hell

VISIONS OF HELL

Eternal torment in the underworld is the fate of sinners in many cultures. The Greeks in particular devised ingenious fates for those who offended the gods. Sisyphus (who told tales on Zeus) was forced to spend eternity rolling a stone uphill, only to see it roll back to the ground just as he was reaching the top. Tantalus (who served the gods his own son at a banquet) was condemned to stand neck-high in water, with ripe fruit dangling over his head, never able to eat or drink.

Norse chieftains were cremated in longboats to transport them to Valhalla

WARRIORS' HEAVEN

Viking warriors longed to be chosen for death in battle by Odin's warrior maidens, the Valkyries. This meant that, instead of going to hell, warriors would experience a glorious afterlife of feasting and fighting in the golden halls of Valhalla. Here they prepare to fight for the gods in the final battle (Ragnarok) of this present world.

White pottery figure of the Aztec lord of death

Sacred sites

THE ICE AGE CAVE pictures of Europe — and their ancient equivalents in Australia, America, and Africa — show us that humankind has always recognized and respected sacred spaces, where the everyday and the eternal meet. Sacred sites may be temporary or permanent, and the same place may be reused many times. Many Christian churches, for instance, are on the sites of pagan temples. Lakes, rivers, caves, woods, or mountaintops may be as spiritual as a temple or church. A place may declare itself sacred simply by its beauty — something the Japanese recognize in erecting *torii* gates (right), in places that are natural shrines. A totem pole, erected to proclaim a family's mythological descent, is also visible proof that the world of humankind and the world of gods and spirits are one and the same.

GREAT PYRAMIDS

The Egyptian sun god Ra was born on a pyramid-shaped piece of land jutting out of the primal ocean. This shape was then adopted by the Egyptian pharaohs (kings) for their tombs, putting them under the protection of the sun god.

Most probably an altar, this flat sandstone block was 16 feet (5 meters) long

STANDING STONES

The building of the great Neolithic temple at Stonehenge in Wiltshire, Great Britain, occurred between about 2500 and 1500 B.C.. The sacred stones, which are aligned with the sun, moon, and stars, are thought to have had astronomical connections. Stonehenge was also adopted as a sacred site by the druids, Celtic priests of the Iron Age (c. 1100 B.C.).

Curved ends of horizontal bars reach toward heaven

GATEWAYS TO HEAVEN

A *torii* is a gateless entranceway that marks the point where ordinary space becomes sacred space. A *torii* stands at the entrance to each Japanese Shinto shrine, and also in front of the sacred Mount Fuji (right). Because *torii* means bird, it is sometimes said that the *torii* is erected to provide a resting place for birds, so that their song will please the gods at dawn.

Thunderbird makes lightning by opening and closing its eyes

The thunderbird creates thunder by flapping its wings

Mythical monuments

The totem poles of North American Indians are carved heraldic monuments displaying images of a family's or clan's mythological descent. Sometimes wealthy families commissioned totem poles as memorials to their dead relatives. The Native American Kwakiutl people say that the first totem pole, *kakaluyuwish* (pole that holds up the sky), was made by Wakiash, a Kwakiutl chief, with knowledge that he won from the animal-people when Raven flew him around the world.

This thunderbird totem pole is among the many historical totem poles that stand in Stanley Park in Vancouver, Canada. *Thunderbird* was copied in 1988 from the original, which was erected in 1927.

TEMPLE OF THE MAIDEN
The word "parthenon" means "temple of the maiden," and the Parthenon was the great temple of Athena situated on the Acropolis at Athens, in Greece. Athena, goddess of war and wisdom, was the patron of the city. The Parthenon contained her statue in gold and ivory and a frieze depicting battle scenes and processions of worshipers.

A human ancestor figure

GOLDEN WATERS
Gold was so important to the Incas that they called it the sweat of the sun god Inti. At El Dorado lake (above) in Colombia, each new king was coated in gold dust before sailing out to throw gold offerings into the water. The Spanish conquerors of Peru heard rumors of this and searched in vain for the kingdom of El Dorado and its fabulous riches.

At sunrise and sunset, Uluru displays spectacular shades of orange and purple

MAJESTIC MOUNTAIN
The sacred site of Uluru, or Ayers Rock, rises from the great natural majesty. The focus of many myths among the Aborigines of central Australia, Uluru was said to have been built in the Dreamtime by two boys playing with mud after rain.

Blade is tied on to the adze with string

D-shaped adze

CARVING TOOLS
Totem poles are carved with simple tools. First the log is roughly hewn with an elbow adze, and then the animal shapes are roughly defined with a D-shaped adze. Deep-cut details are achieved with curved knives.

Curved knives

Elbow adze

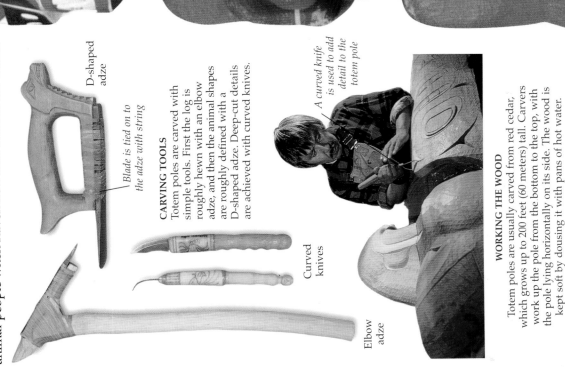

A curved knife is used to add detail to the totem pole

WORKING THE WOOD
Totem poles are usually carved from red cedar, which grows up to 200 feet (60 meters) tall. Carvers work up the pole from the bottom to the top, with the pole lying horizontally on its side. The wood is kept soft by dousing it with pans of hot water.

End of the world

JUST AS MYTHOLOGIES TELL how the world began, so they predict how it will end, often in a terrible fire or flood. The Aborigines of southeastern Australia believed that the end would come when one of the four props that held up the sky rotted away, allowing the sky to fall. The Native American Cherokee believed that the world was a great floating island, held by four cords hanging down from the sky, and that when these rotted through, the Earth would sink back beneath the sea. The ancient Egyptians, who feared every night that the sun god would be defeated in his journey through the underworld and fail to reappear, also foresaw a time when the god would grow so old and tired that he would forget who he was, so that all he had created would come to an end.

The world will end when the rainbow serpent chews his own tail

COSMIC SERPENT
In West Africa Aido-Hwedo, the rainbow snake, carried the creator in his mouth while the world was made, and then circled around the Earth to hold it together. Red monkeys beneath the sea forge iron bars to feed him. When the iron runs out, Aido-Hwedo will chew his own tail, the world will convulse, and the Earth and all its burdens will slide into the sea.

Rocky matter from an explosion in space

The world serpent has many heads

When Brahma awakes, he rises on a lotus flower from the god Vishnu

Lakshmi, Vishnu's wife, the goddess of fortune

At night Vishnu rests on the world serpent, Shesha

END OF THE KALPA
For Hindus, time is an endless cycle of days and nights of Brahma, or kalpas. During the day, when Brahma is awake, the world is created anew; when Brahma goes to sleep, the kalpa ends. Each kalpa lasts 4.32 billion years.

GREAT WORLD POLE

According to the Native American Cheyenne people, the Great White Grandfather Beaver of the North is gnawing the great pole that holds up the world. When he gnaws right through, the world will end. The Tsimshian of the northwest coast say that the pole on which the world spins is held up by Amala. He has a servant who gives him strength by rubbing his back with wild-duck oil once a year. The oil is nearly used up; when it runs out, Amala will die, and the world will fall.

North American family totem (symbol) of the beaver

MYTH OF THE FIVE SUNS

The Aztecs believed that this world was the fifth, and that each creation had its own sun. The fifth sun first shone on August 13, 3114 B.C., and will last until at least A.D. 4772. But it will not last forever, for "all moons, all years, all days, all winds, reach their completion and pass away."

Aztec calendar stone c. 1352

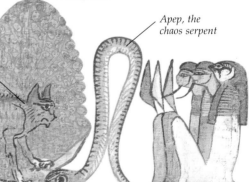

The Sun god Ra in the guise of a cat

Apep, the chaos serpent

EGYPTIAN APEP

Each night, as the sun god Ra voyaged through the underworld, his ship was attacked by the chaos serpent Apep, his mortal enemy. If Apep ever devoured Ra, the world would end. Each night Ra took the form of a cat and cut off Apep's head.

THE BIG CRUNCH

Many mythologies envisage a cycle of creation and destruction and foresee the emergence of a new world after this one ends. According to scientific theory, this is perfectly feasible. The universe, which is currently expanding, may one day reach a maximum size and collapse in on itself in a "Big Crunch." The matter and energy from the collapsed universe may then bounce back to create a new universe.

LAST BATTLE OF THE NORSE GODS

The warlike Vikings thought the world would end in a final cataclysmic battle, in which all the main gods would die and the Earth would be consumed by fire. This battle is Ragnarok, the twilight of the gods. The wolf Fenrir, child of the trickster Loki, will break his bonds, kill Odin the all-father, and swallow the sun. But from this world's ruin, a new creation will arise.

Midgard serpent — monstrous child of the trickster Loki

Did you know?

MYTH AND FACT

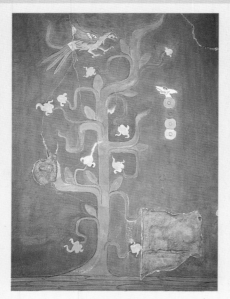

A Mexican Tree of Life

The Sphinx was a mythical monster sent to punish the Thebans. She gobbled up anyone who could not solve her riddle: "What walks on four legs, then two legs, and then three?" The answer was Man. He crawls on all fours as a baby, then walks upright on two legs, then has a third "leg" in old age – his walking stick.

The Canaanites had a grisly way of placating their thunder god, Baal. When they built a new house, a couple sacrificed a young child and buried it under the foundations.

Archaeologists have unearthed evidence to explain the trances of the Pythia – the priestess at Delphi in ancient Greece. Ethylene gas was escaping from faults in the rock and this would have made the Pythia hallucinate. In her trance, she believed the god Apollo spoke to her.

According to an old Indian legend, the coastal town of Mahabalipuram in southern India once had seven beautiful temples – until the gods sent a flood to destroy the town. Today, only one temple stands on the seashore, but in 2002, divers found exciting evidence of six more temples under the sea.

A butterfly, symbol of the Pima creator god

The Pima Indians thought the creator god, Great Butterfly, flew down and made the first people from his own sweat. Across the Pacific, a tribe on Sumatra believed its ancestors had hatched from butterfly eggs.

One West African myth tells how the Earth mother, Iyadola, made the first people from clay. Some were white, because they were not fired enough. Some were fired too long and burned black. Others came out yellow, brown, or pink.

Leprechauns are creatures of Irish folklore. If caught by a human, they have to reveal the whereabouts of their hoard of gold.

Some modern Mexican artists create extraordinarily intricate images of the Tree of Life. They incorporate gods and other figures from Mayan and Aztec mythologies, combined with symbols borrowed from the Catholic Church.

On the Indonesian island of Java, *wayang-kulit* (shadow-puppet) plays enact traditional myths. Behind the cloth screen, the puppeteer operates the puppets with wires or rods. The audience sees their shadows projected onto the screen. Shows can last up to nine hours.

Javanese *wayang kulit* made from leather

The Giant's Causeway on the Antrim coast in Northern Ireland is named after the giant Finn MacCool. According to legend, Finn built a causeway of huge stepping stones across the sea to Scotland. In reality, volcanic activity formed the hexagonal basalt stones about 60 million years ago.

Part of the Giant's Causeway in Northern Ireland

In 2001 an archaeologist discovered the earliest known picture of the Mayan corn god. The mural, found in Guatemala, was painted around 100 C.E. According to Mayan myth, the corn god went to the underworld but was later resurrected. Like the Greek story of Demeter, this story explained the seasons and harvest.

One Greek myth tells how Leto (mother of Artemis and Apollo) turned some nasty peasants into frogs. The peasants did not want her to drink from their lake, so they muddied the water with sticks. To punish them, Leto decided they should stay croaking in the mud forever.

There are many versions of the tale of how Arthur became King of the Britons. In one, Arthur proved his right to kingship by drawing Excalibur, an enchanted sword, from a stone. In another, the Lady of the Lake gave him the sword.

In Norse mythology, a terrible serpent was thought to lie coiled around the world at the bottom of the sea. Later, Norwegian sailors believed in the kraken, a many-armed sea monster that was 1.5 miles (2.4 km) across and capable of pulling a ship down into the sea.

QUESTIONS AND ANSWERS

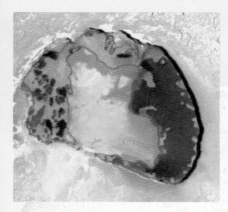

Tupan Patera crater on Jupiter's moon, Io, photographed from the *Galileo* spacecraft

Q Do any of the planets have mythical associations?

A All of the planets in our solar system, apart from Earth, are named after gods or goddesses. These are taken from the Roman pantheon (family of gods) with one exception – Uranus was the primordial sky god in Greek myth. The remaining seven planets are named after Mercury, speedy messenger of the gods; Venus, goddess of love; Mars, god of farming and war; Jupiter, king of the gods; Saturn, god of the heavens; Neptune, god of water; and Pluto, god of the underworld.

Q Do any other landmarks in our solar system have mythical names?

A Many of the moons are named after characters from myths. The Martian moons Phobos and Deimos, for example, take their names from two of the sons of Ares, the Greek god of war. Jupiter's four largest moons are called Ganymede, Callisto, Io, and Europa. These are all the names of characters from Greek myth, whom Zeus kidnapped or seduced. Io, for example, was a beautiful nymph, but Zeus turned her into a cow to hide her from his jealous wife, Hera. Astronomers recently discovered a volcanic crater on Io, and that too has a mythical name – Tupan Patera, named after the Brazilian thunder god. It is about 47 miles (75 km) across and extremely active.

Temple of Kukulkan in Mexico

Q How does a Sami shaman drum up the spirit world?

A The Sami people live in northern Europe, across the countries of Finland, Norway, Sweden, and Russia. In some areas, they are still able to live as they have done for hundreds of years. Traditionally, each tribe has a shaman called a *noaide* who looks after the people's physical and spiritual health. He can also cast spells and tell prophecies. The shaman summons up the spirit world by entering a trance. To do this, he performs special rituals that include beating a magic drum called a *runebom*.

Q Which pyramid spoke in the voice of a god?

A Many experts agree that the Mayan Temple of Kukulkan at Chichén Itzá, Mexico, produces echoes that sound like the cry of a quetzal bird – though not all are convinced the pyramid's acoustics were intentional. The quetzal was sacred to the Maya. It was linked to their god Kukulkan, the "quetzal serpent," the equivalent of the Aztec god Quetzalcoatl. If a priest had stood at the base of the temple steps and clapped, the pyramid would have "answered" in the divine quetzal's voice. The pyramid also has another special effect: Around sunset during the spring and fall equinoxes, a shadow travels up or down the staircase. Its shape looks like the quetzal serpent god! Some experts think that special ceremonies were held at the equinoxes, when Mayan worshippers could see the shadow and hear the echo at the same time.

Q Which animal links the Kongo world with the next?

A The Kongo people live in Central Africa. In traditional rituals, they use carved objects called *nkisi* to call up the spirits. *Nkisi* are hollow so they can be filled with magical herbs. One popular *nkisi* is Kozo, the dog. The Kongo believe dogs inhabit both the land of the living (the village) and the land of the dead (the forest where they hunt). The Kozo ritual figure usually has two heads, one to face each realm.

Kongo carving of Kozo
(late 1800s)

Record Breakers

OLDEST MYTHICAL PAINTINGS
Cave art found at Chauvet-Pont-d'Arc, France, dates back 31,000 years. It includes hundreds of animal figures and probably depicts important myths.

OLDEST MYTHICAL STORY
Parts of the *Epic of Gilgamesh* have been found on clay fragments dating from around 1700 B.C.E., but the story itself originated earlier – around 3000 B.C.E.

OLDEST ANCIENT WONDER
The Great Pyramid at Giza, Egypt, is the oldest survivor of the seven wonders of the ancient world. It was built around 4,500 years ago.

DIVINE STATUE
A statue of Vulcan cast for the 1904 World's Fair in St. Louis stood 50 ft (15.25 m) high.

Mythical meanings

Lotus flower

IN MYTHS AND LEGENDS, elements from the natural world frequently take on a symbolic meaning. Often, a single symbol will have different meanings in different cultures and mythologies. Here are just a few of the meanings attached to some plants, including flowers and fruits.

APPLE
The Norse gods ate the golden apples of Idun, goddess of spring, to stay young. There were golden apples in Greek mythology, too: The hero Hercules managed to steal them as one of his Twelve Labors, but first he had to kill Ladon, the 100-headed dragon that was guarding them.

ASH
Yggdrasil, the world tree of Norse mythology, was a mighty ash. The Vikings believed that the first people were carved from ash wood. In the Middle Ages, people sometimes fed their babies ash sap – it was thought to repel witches.

Cherries

CHERRY
The Chinese considered the cherry tree to be lucky and a symbol of spring. In Japan, samurai warriors used the cherry fruit as their emblem, possibly because its blood-colored flesh hid a tough, strong heart.

DATE
In the deserts of North Africa and the Middle East, the date has always been an important source of food and is often linked with fertility. The Egyptians associated the date palm with the Tree of Life, and pictures of date palms decorate their temples and shrines.

FIG
The Romans believed that their god of wine, Bacchus, created the fig. They also believed that their city's founders, Romulus and Remus, had been suckled under the shade of a fig tree on the banks of the Tiber River.

IRIS
The iris is the namesake of the Greek rainbow goddess. In Japanese folklore, irises protected homes from evil spirits.

IVY
The Greek god Dionysus was found under an ivy bush as a baby. He was often shown crowned with ivy and carrying an ivy-entwined staff. Ivy has also come to stand for longevity, perhaps because in nature ivy can keep on growing after its host tree has died.

Trailing ivy

JUJUBE TREE
The Taoists hold that the fruit of the jujube tree was the food of the gods. The tree's spiny branches are sometimes believed to have protective powers.

LAUREL
The laurel was associated with the Greek god Apollo. Daphne, the nymph he fell in love with, was turned into a laurel to escape him, and he wore a laurel-leaf crown ever after. The Pythia at Delphi may have chewed laurel leaves during her trances in order to get closer to the god. Victorious Roman generals also wore laurel wreaths. In Chinese myth, the elixir of immortality was mixed beneath a laurel tree.

LILY
The lily was associated with the Greek goddess Hera – it was said to have sprung from her milk. Elsewhere it has served as a symbol of purity or prosperity.

An ancient Egyptian painting showing a date palm

LOTUS
Lotus flowers made up the crown of Osiris, the ancient Egyptian god of the underworld. The flower was an emblem of rebirth because of the way it rose up from the muddy bed of the Nile. The lotus is also important to the Hindu and Buddhist faiths as a symbol of earth and creation.

MAIZE
The Aztecs worshipped several maize, or corn, gods, and the plant was important to North American Indians too, as a symbol of harvest and abundance. The Greeks and Romans worshipped their own grain goddesses – Demeter and Ceres.

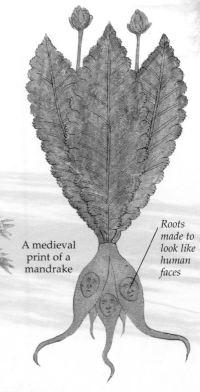

A medieval print of a mandrake

Roots made to look like human faces

MANDRAKE
The mandrake was once thought to have magical powers because of its roots, which often resemble human figures. The plant was said to scream when uprooted – and the sound was loud enough to kill a person! In Greek myth, the sorceress Circe used mandrake root in her spells.

MARIGOLD
The Chinese associate this bright orange flower with the sun and longevity. In India, it is the sacred flower of Krishna.

MUSHROOM
The Greeks associated the mushroom with ambrosia, the food of the gods. In European folklore, mushrooms and toadstools became associated with fairies and pixies, perhaps because of the way they spring up overnight, as if by magic.

A watercolor painting of a myrtle branch

MYRTLE
With its evergreen leaves and sweet scent, myrtle was linked with the Greek goddess of love, Aphrodite. It came to be a symbol of marital love and childbirth. In China, the plant was associated with success.

NARCISSUS
In Greek mythology, Narcissus was a beautiful youth who fell in love with his own reflection. Since he was unable to move from the pool's edge, he eventually faded away. As a result, the narcissus flower is often seen as a symbol of early death. It was also the spring flower that Persephone was gathering when Hades came by in his chariot and carried her off to the underworld.

Narcissus flowers

OAK
Traditionally, the oak has been important across Europe, representing might and longevity. In Greek mythology, Hercules's club was made of oak wood and so was Jason's ship, the *Argo*. According to the Romans, the sky god Jupiter was sheltered under an oak as an infant. The Druids often held their sacred rites under oak trees.

OLIVE
Olives were important to all the ancient civilizations around the Mediterranean as a source of oil as well as food. In Greek myth, the goddess Athena first made the olive bear fruit in order to convince the citizens of Attica, the region around Athens, to choose her as their leader, instead of the sea god, Poseidon, who offered them only a horse. The Japanese consider the olive to be a symbol of friendship and success.

PLUM
In China, the plum tree is associated with happy marriages and longevity, partly because it blooms so early. The great Chinese philosopher Lao-tse was said to have been born under a plum tree.

POMEGRANATE
The pomegranate is a symbol of fertility. While Persephone was in the underworld with Hades, she ate some pomegranate seeds – this condemned her to spend four months of every year in the underworld.

Poppy

POPPY
Traditionally, the poppy is an emblem of sleep, death, and the soothing of pain, because of the properties of opium, which is found in poppies. The bright red of the flower's petals have also made it a symbol of blood and slaughter.

ROSE
In Roman myth, the red rose sprang from the blood of the love goddess, Venus. She had caught her foot on the thorn of a white rose while running to the side of her dying lover, Adonis. Venus's son, Cupid, used a rose to bribe the god of silence when he wanted to put a stop to gossip about his mother.

ROSEMARY
The herb rosemary is known to have healing powers, but in European folklore it was used to protect against witches, fairies, evil spirits, and even storms. The Romans associated it with the goddess Venus.

The goddess Athena

TAMARISK
The tamarisk is a desert-growing tree that produces edible resin. In ancient Egypt, it was associated with the god Osiris. The Chinese held the tamarisk to be a symbol of immortality, and the Japanese associated it with life-giving rain.

VINE
The grapevine is the source of wine, and it was therefore linked with the Greek god Dionysus and the Roman god Bacchus. Followers of these gods drank wine to bring themselves into closer contact with the divine. Bunches of grapes often symbolized fruitfulness and plenty, but they could also suggest drunkenness.

WILLOW
The Ainu people of Japan believed that a willow branch formed the spine of the first man. The Chinese associated it with strength and flexibility.

YEW
The yew tree lives to a great age, so it mostly appears as a symbol of immortality. The Druids used to make their wands and bows out of yew wood. It was considered very unlucky to cut down a yew.

Find out more

MYTHOLOGY IS ALL AROUND YOU – so much so that sometimes you may not even notice it. Creatures of ancient myth pop up in modern stories, for example, and in many movies. You can also find books or Web sites that retell classical myths. In art galleries and museums, you can see paintings that depict fascinating stories of gods and heroes, as well as sacred artifacts and clothing that has played a part in the storytelling of peoples from all over the world. Finally, you may even find that some of the festivals and traditions you observe are rooted in ancient myths.

AMPHITHEATER ON THE ACROPOLIS, ATHENS, GREECE
Ancient Greek playwrights drew on their rich heritage of myths. Many of their works are still performed today in theaters around the world. One of the most amazing places to see a Greek play is in an ancient amphitheater. The Theater of Herodes Atticus was built around 161 C.E. Performances are staged there each summer as part of the Athens Festival.

MYTHOLOGY AT THE MOVIES
Filmmakers often look to myths to find plots for their films. *Jason and the Argonauts*, made in 1963, charts the quest of the Greek hero Jason for the Golden Fleece. In the movie, Jason slays the dragon guarding the fleece and also faces many other thrilling dangers. He defeats harpies and tames fire-snorting bulls. He even manages to steer his ship through two moving cliffs that usually crush anything that passes.

The sea god, Poseidon

Jason's ship was the Argo, so his crew were known as the Argonauts

STANDING STONES AT CARNAC, FRANCE
Many ancient sacred sites can still be seen in the landscape. Visiting one of these is a good way to get closer to the people who created the earliest myths and stories. At Carnac, in southern Brittany, there are more than 3,000 stone monuments. They have been standing there for 6,000 years – since the Stone Age.

CORN DOLLY
Perhaps you have seen or even made a corn dolly. Traditionally, this was made with the last sheaf of the wheat harvest, and kept safe because it housed the spirit of the wheat.

BACCHUS AND ARIADNE (1521–23) BY TITIAN
If you are lucky enough to visit London's National Gallery, you may see this painting by Titian. It depicts Bacchus, the Roman god of wine, when he first sees the princess Ariadne. He turned her crown into stars, so Titian painted stars twinkling in the sky above Ariadne's head.

HALLOWEEN SPOOKS
Halloween has its roots in Celtic rituals. The festival Samhain, held on November 1, honored the Celtic Lord of the Dead. The night before, he assembled all the wicked souls who had died in the past year.

USEFUL WEB SITES

- An online encyclopedia of mythology and folklore
  www.pantheon.org/mythica.html
- Resources on mythologies from different world cultures
  www.gods-heros-myth.com
- Guide to gods, heroes, and monsters of Greek myth
  www.mythweb.com
- Information on Egyptian gods from the British Museum
  www.ancientegypt.co.uk/gods
- Stories about Saxon and Viking gods
  www.gwydir.demon.co.uk/jo/nordic

Places to visit

PHILADELPHIA MUSEUM OF ART, PHILADELPHIA, PENNSYLVANIA
(215) 763-8100
www.philamuseum.org
One treasure is the Pillared Hall from a Hindu Temple (or Mandapa), with its life-size figures of heroes, sages, mythical animals, and divine beings that relate to Vishnu and his appearances on Earth in human and animal form. Carved panels show scenes from the Ramayana, the great Indian epic based on the exploits of Rama, one of Vishnu's manifestations on earth.

METROPOLITAN MUSEUM OF ART, NEW YORK, NEW YORK
(212) 535-7710
www.metmuseum.org
Built around 15 B.C.E. and transported to the Met in 1934, the Temple of Dendur is a small temple honoring the goddess Isis, as well as Pedesi and Pihor, deified sons of a local Nubian chieftain. The museum is also home to thousands of other myth-related works of art from Egypt, Greece, India, Africa, and the rest of the world.

THE GETTY CENTER, LOS ANGELES, CALIFORNIA
(310) 440-7300
www.getty.edu
An extensive collection of myth-related art is highlighted by Giovanni Battista Foggini's *Laocoön*, a bronze of the ancient marble statue found in 1506. In Greek mythology, the Trojan prince Laocoön angered Apollo by breaking a vow of celibacy and warning the Trojans not to bring the Greeks' wooden horse into the city. To silence him, Apollo sent serpents to kill him and his sons.

SMITHSONIAN INSTITUTION, WASHINGTON, D.C.
(202) 633-1000
www.si.edu
Parent organization for the African Art Museum, the National Museum of the American Indian, Latino Initiatives, the Asian Pacific American program, and the Center for Folklife and Cultural Heritage. Its collection includes more than 140 million works of art.

BASTET THE CAT GODDESS
If you want to come face-to-face with an ancient god, visit a museum. This statue of the Egyptian goddess Bastet is on display in the Louvre in Paris. Many large museums have collections of objects that will help you find out more about ancient myths and the people who created them.

Glossary

ADZE An axlike cutting tool

AFTERLIFE A life after death

AMULET A charm believed to have magical powers and worn to bring luck or ward off evil spirits

ANCESTOR Someone from whom a person is descended

ARCHAEOLOGIST Someone who studies artifacts made by humans long ago

AVATAR The appearance of a Hindu god in physical form

BIG BANG The huge explosion that created the Universe around 13,000 million years ago

BODHISATTVA A Buddhist saint worthy of nirvana who remains with humans in order to help them.

Krishna, an avatar of Vishnu

BOOMERANG A curved throwing weapon used by Australian Aborigines

BREASTPLATE A piece of armor that protects the chest

CATACLYSMIC Describes something that is – or causes – a total disaster

CENTAUR A mythical creature, half man and half horse

CHIMERA A mythical fire-breathing monster with a lion's head, goat's body, and serpent's tail

A model of the Chimera

COSMOLOGY The study or explanation of order in the universe

COSMOS The whole world or universe, seen to be arranged according to a particular pattern or order.

CULT A group of believers who are intensely devoted to one spiritual leader or divine figure

CYCLOPS A one-eyed giant from Greek mythology

DEITY A god or goddess

DEMON A devil or evil spirit

DISMEMBERED Describes a body that has been torn limb from limb

DIVINE Of or like a god

DRAGON A mythical, fire-breathing monster with a huge scaly body, wings, claws, and a tail. In Chinese myth, dragons are wingless, benevolent beings that live in water and the sky.

DREAMTIME The eternal present in which the sacred ancestors of the Australian Aborigines shaped human beings and the world. Aboriginal myths take place in the Dreamtime, which can be re-entered by ritual, song, and dance.

DRUID A Celtic priest

ECSTASY A trancelike state of heightened joy

ELIXIR A liquid possessing magical powers, such as the granting of immortality

FERTILITY The ability to produce children or grow crops

GORGON In Greek mythology, one of three monstrous, serpent-haired sisters – Stheno, Euryale, and Medusa

GRIFFIN A mythical creature, half eagle, half lion

HEADHUNTER A tribal warrior who collects the heads of his victims as trophies

IMMORTAL A being that will never die

INCARNATION The appearance of a god in physical form

INITIATED Accepted or admitted into a group – or a certain part of society – usually after going through certain important rites

Painted lotus-shaped tiles from an ancient Egyptian temple

KALPA In Hindu cosmology, a period in which the universe experiences one cycle of creation (when Brahma is awake) and destruction (when Brahma sleeps)

KATHAKALI A classical dance-drama from Kerala, southern India, usually performed by men and boys. Dancers mime to a sung story from a Hindu epic, such as the *Ramayana* or the *Mahabharata*.

KAYAK A sealskin canoe used by the Inuit

LAVA Hot molten rock that erupts from a volcano or an opening in the Earth's crust

Map of Mesoamerica

LONGEVITY Living for a long time

LOTUS A water lily growing in Egypt or India

MACE A ceremonial staff or war club

MERGED Joined or blended together

MESOAMERICA Ancient region of Central America, comprising central and southern Mexico and the Yucatan Peninsula, Guatemala, Belize, El Salvador, western Honduras, and parts of Nicaragua and Costa Rica. Before the 16th-century Spanish conquest, Mesoamerica was home to civilizations such as the Aztecs and Maya.

MILKY WAY Our galaxy, a family of star systems held together by gravity, which contains our own solar system

MORTAL A being that will live for a limited time and then die

MUMMIFIED Describes a body that has been turned into a mummy – preserved so that it will not decay

MYTH A story about gods or heroes that often explains how the world came to be as it is or how people should live in it. In everyday speech the word "myth" is sometimes used to mean an untruth.

NEOLITHIC The New Stone Age, which began around the time of the last ice age. Neolithic people used more complex stone tools, built stone structures, and began to make pottery.

NIRVANA In Buddhism and Hinduism, the state of supreme happiness and enlightenment – awareness of the true nature of human existence

NYMPH In Greek mythology, a beautiful young woman who usually has one divine parent. Nereids and oceanids were sea nymphs, naiads were water nymphs, oreads were mountain nymphs, and dryads were tree nymphs.

ORACLE Either a place where the words of a god are revealed or the person through whom a god speaks

PAGAN A person who follows a religion other than Christianity, Judaism, or Islam

PEGASUS A mythical winged horse

PHARAOH The title given to the rulers of ancient Egypt. The word means "great house" and originally referred to the king's palace rather than the king.

PIGMENT The chemicals that give a thing its coloring. In their sacred sandpaintings, Navajos use pigments made from plants and minerals.

PRIMORDIAL Existing at or from the very beginning of creation

PROSPERITY Having good fortune, money, and success

PYRAMID A massive stone structure with a square base and sloping sides. These could be royal tombs, as in Egypt, or sacrificial temples, as in Mesoamerica.

REINCARNATION The belief that a dead person is reborn in another body

An Aztec sacrificial knife

Ritual mask worn by an African shaman

RESURRECTION Rising from the dead or being restored to life

RITE A religious or spiritual ceremony

RITUAL A formalized set of actions and words in which gods are worshipped or asked for help

SACRED Holy or revered

SACRIFICE An offering made to please or placate a god, usually at a cost to the giver. A sacrifice can be a slaughtered animal or even a human being.

SHAMAN A priest or medicine man, whose role is to look after the health and spiritual welfare of the tribe. He does this by carrying out and presiding over special rituals that will influence good or evil spirits.

SHRINE A sacred place dedicated to or associated with a god, spirit, or holy object

SOOTHSAYING Telling fortunes or predicting the future

SORCEROR A wizard or magician who casts spells and has magic powers

SPIRIT A bodiless person or being

SUPERNATURAL Magical or spiritual and beyond the laws of nature

TORII The entrance to a Shinto temple. Usually painted red, it consists of two vertical wooden posts, topped with two horizontal beams, of which the topmost extends beyond the supports.

TOTEM Native American name for a spiritual ancestor. A totem can be a living creature, for example an eagle, or an inanimate thing, such as a river.

TRIBE A group of people who are often related and share the same language and culture

TRICKSTER A person or god who plays tricks or deceives

TSUNAMI A huge sea wave, usually triggered by a volcano or earthquake

UNDERWORLD Mythical region below the Earth where people are said to live after death

UNICORN A mythical horse with a spiral horn on its forehead

VALHALLA In Norse mythology, the great hall of Odin, where dead heroes spend the afterlife, feasting and fighting

VALKYRIE In Norse mythology, one of the female battle spirits who guide heroes to Valhalla

VISION A mystical or religious experience in which a person sees a god or spirit

YANG (*see also* YIN) In Chinese philosophy, one of the two complementary principles. Yang is positive, active, bright, warm, and masculine.

YIN (*see also* YANG) In Chinese philosophy, one of the two complementary principles. Yin is negative, passive, dark, cold, and feminine.

This ornate Viking stone, found on the Swedish island of Gotland, shows a Norse warrior riding into Valhalla

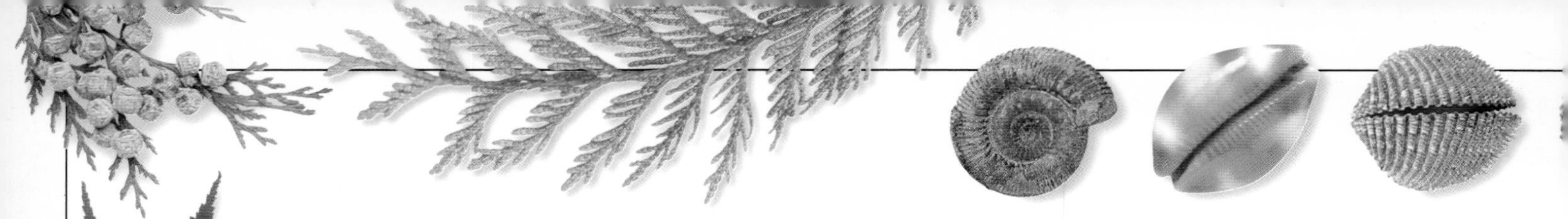

72-page Eyewitness Titles

American Revolution
Ancient Egypt
Ancient Greece
Ancient Rome
Arms & Armor
Astronomy
Baseball
Basketball
Bird
Castle
Cat
Crystal & Gem
Dance
Dinosaur
Dog
Early Humans
Earth
Explorer
Fish
Flying Machine
Food
Fossil
Future
Horse

Human Body
Hurricane & Tornado
Insect
Islam
Invention
Jungle
Knight
Mammal
Mars
Medieval Life
Mummy
Music
Mythology
NASCAR
North American Indian
Ocean
Olympics
Photography
Pirate
Plant

Pond & River
Pyramid
Religion
Rocks & Minerals
Seashore
Shakespeare
Shark
Shipwreck
Skeleton
Soccer
Space Exploration
Titanic
Tree
Vietnam
Viking
Volcano & Earthquake
Weather
Whale
Wild West
World War I
World War II

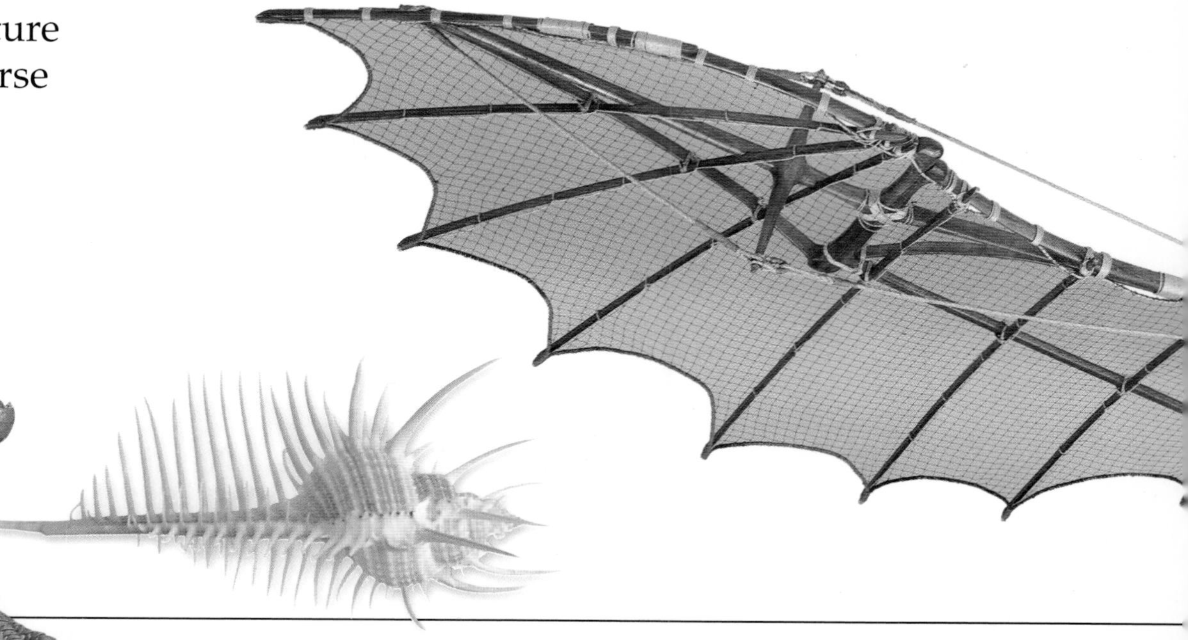

Other Eyewitness Titles

Index

Acknowledgments

The publisher would like to thank: Alan Hills, Philip Nicholls, Christi Graham, John Williams, Kevin Lovelock, Jim Rossiter, and Janet Peckham of the British Museum, London; Kalamandalam Vijayakumar and Kalamandalam Barbara Vijayakumar; and the African Crafts Centre, Covent Garden, London.

Photography: Andy Crawford
Researcher: Robert Graham
Index: Chris Bernstein
Design assistance: Jill Bunyan and Anna Martin

Picture credits
The publisher would like to thank the following for their kind permission to reproduce the photographs:
(t=top, b=bottom, a=above, c=center, l=left, r=right)

AKG Images: 39tr, 39l; Boymans van Beuningen Museum, Rotterdam *The Tower of Babel*, Pieter Brueghel the Elder 9r; Erich Lessing/Württembergisches Landesmuseum, Stuttgart 9bcr, 26tl, 46tl; SMPK Kupferstichkabinett, Berlin 14tl; Torquil Cramer 58/59c; Universitets Oldsaksamling, Oslo 34bc; Von der Heydt Museum, Wuppertal Flora, *Awakening Flowers*, 1876, by Arnold Bücklin (1827–1901) 25bl. **American Museum of Natural History:** 43br, 50tr, 52cl; Thos. Beiswenger 41r. **Ancient Art & Architecture Collection:** 60tl; D.F. Head 31tr; Ronald Sheridan 10bl, 13br, 23cl, 26br, 27ar, 45l, 45ca. **The Art Archive:** Buonconsiglio Castle Trento/Dagli Orti 62cr; Musée du Louvre Paris/Dagli Orti 65br; National Gallery London/Eileen Tweedy 65c; Dagli

Orti 61bc, 62bc; Mireille Vautier 60bl. **Ashmolean Museum, Oxford:** 16c, 32br, 42/43c. **Duncan Baird Publishers Archive:** 16tl; Japanese Gallery 11cr, 33c. **Bildarchiv Preußischer Kulturbesitz:** 34tl; SMPK Berlin 18; Staatliche Museum, Berlin 48tr. **Bridgeman Art Library, London/New York:** British Museum, London *The Weighing of the Heart Against Maat's Feather of Truth*, Egyptian, early 19th Dynasty, c.1300 B.C.E., *Book of the Dead of the Royal Scribe* 54br; By Courtesy of the Board of the Trustees of the V&A *Vishnu in the Centre of his Ten Avatars*, Jaipur area, 18th century 20tl; Galleria degli Uffizi, Florence, Italy *The Birth of Venus*, c.1485, by Sandro Botticelli (1444/5–1510) 42cl; Louvre, Paris, France/Giraudon *Stele of a Woman before Re-Harakhy*, Egyptian, c.1000BC 15tl; Musée Condé, Chantilly, France MS 860/401 f.7 *The Story of Adam and Eve*, detail from "Cas des Nobles Hommes et Femmes" by Boccaccio, translated by Laurent de Premierfait, French 1465, *Works of Giovanni Boccaccio* (1313–75) 9bl (right), 17br; Museo Correr, Venice, Italy *Glimpse of Hell* (panel) by Flemish School (15th century) 55bl; Piazza della Signoria, Florence/Lauros – Giraudon *Perseus with the Head of a Medusa*, 1545–54, in the Loggia dei Lanzi, by Benvenuto Cellini (1500–71) 35bcr; Private Collection Genesis 6:11-24 Noah's Ark, Nuremberg Bible (Biblia Sacra Germanaica), 1483 21cb. **British Museum, London:** 6br, 6bl, 9bc, 13tr, 14tr, 16r, 17c, 17r, 17tr, 18tr, 19r, 23t, 25tl, 28bl, 31br, 35tr, 36c, 38br, 39br, 42tl, 43tc, 43tr, 52bl, 53tl. **Cambridge Museum of Anthropology:** 21r, 57tr. **Central Art Archives:** The Old Students House, Helsinki 19tl. **Jean-Loup Charmet:** 9tr, 21tl. **Christie's Images:** *In the Well of the Great Wave of Kanagawa*, c.1797, by Hokusai

Katsushika (1760–1849) 20/21b, 30r, 31l. **Bruce Coleman Ltd:** Jeff Foott Productions 44tl. **Corbis:** 68-69; Chinch Gryniewicz/Ecoscene 62-63; Michael S. Yamashita 64-65. **CM Dixon:** 31bc. **DK Picture Library:** American Museum of Natural History/Lynton Gardiner 67tc; British Museum 66tr; Glasgow Museum 66tcl; INAH/Michel Zabé 67bl; Statens Historika Museum, Stockholm 67br. **Edimedia:** 14cr. **E.T. Archive:** 33l; British Library Or 13805 56bl; Freer Gallery of Art 24br; Victoria & Albert Museum, London 12/13c. **Mary Evans Picture Library:** 12bl, 12br, 23bl, 28c, 30tl, 32bl. **Werner Forman Archive:** Anthropology Museum, Veracruz University, Jalapa 55r; Arhus Kunstmuseum, Denmark 32cl; Dallas Museum of Art 28bl; David Bernstein Fine Art, New York 51r; Field Museum of Natural History, Chicago 11t; Museum of the American Indian, Heye Foundation 15cl; Smithsonian Institution 14bl; State Museum of Berlin 18cl. **Glasgow Museums (St Mungo):** 33bl, 34bl, 40bl, 50br, 54tr. **Ronald Grant Archive:** Columbia Pictures 64bc. **Hamburgisches Museum für Völkerkunde:** 45tr. **Heritage Image Partnership:** James Sowerby 63cla. **Michael Holford:** British Museum 9cr (below), 10bc, 10tl, 15bl, 16bl, 42bl, 57cr; Kunisada 15br; Museum of Mankind 44bl; Victoria & Albert Museum, London 11br. **Hutchison Library:** Ian Lloyd 59br. **Images Colour Library:** 26c, 57br, 58tr; Impact: Mark Henley 59tr. **INAH/Michael Zabe:** 21tc, 24l, 18bc. **Barnabas Kindersley:** 55tl, 55ca; **Lonely Planet Images:** George Tsafos 64tr. **MacQuitty International Photo Collection:** 41bl. **Nilesh Mistry:** 32tl. **Musée de L'Homme, France:** 22l; D Ponsard 38l, 56tl. **Museum of Anthropology, Vancouver:** 59cl.

Museum of Mankind: 6cl, 34c, 37tc. **NASA:** 61tl. **National Maritime Museum:** 4c, 49tr. **National Museum of Copenhagen:** 36/37b. **The Board of Trustees of the National Museums & Galleries on Merseyside:** 30bl, 53tr. **Natural History Museum, London:** 4tcl, 29tr, 29c, 48/49b, 48tl, 49tl, 49r, 66bl. © **David Neel, 1998:** 4tl. **Peter Newark's Pictures:** 8br, 18r, 41cl, 51c. **Panos Pictures:** Caroline Penn 59bl. **Ann & Bury Peerless:** 22cl, 47tl. **Pitt Rivers Museum, Oxford:** 8bcl, 12tr, 25cr, 40tr, 53bl; Zither 19tc. **Planet Earth Pictures:** Jan Tove Johansson 10l. **Axel Poignant Archive:** 13cl, 23br, 37tl. **Rex Features:** Tim Brooke 55bcl. **Rijksmuseum voor Volkenkunde:** 22r. **Réunion des Musées Nationaux Agence Photographique:** Hervé Lewandowski 28tl, 35cr; Richard Lambert 39cbr. **Royal Ontario Museum:** 63tr. **Science Photo Library:** Chris Bjornerg 10/11c; Sally Benusen (1982) 56/57c. **South American Pictures:** Tony Morrison 15tr, 59cr. **Spectrum Colour Library:** 58cr. **Statens Historika Museum, Stockholm:** 9br. **Oliver Strewe:** 52cr; 31cra. **Topham Picturepoint:** 60cr, 61cra, 65tl.

Jacket credits: Front cover: Tl: Natural History Museum, UK; Tcl: Pitt Rivers Museum, UK; B: John Prior Images/Alamy.

All other images © Dorling Kindersley
For more information see: www.dkimages.com